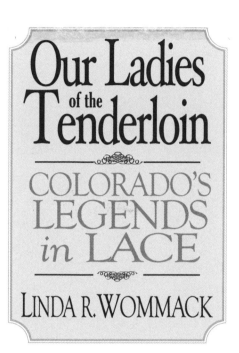

Our Ladies of the Tenderloin

COLORADO'S LEGENDS in LACE

LINDA R. WOMMACK

Our Ladies of the Tenderloin
COLORADO'S LEGENDS IN LACE

By

Linda R. Wommack

CAXTON PRESS

2005

ISBN 0-87004-444-3

Library of Congress Cataloging-in-Publication Data

Wommack, Linda, 1958-

Our ladies of the tenderloin : Colorado's legends in lace / by Linda R. Wommack.

p. cm.

ISBN 0-87004-444-3

1. Prostitution—Colorado—History. 2. Frontier and pioneer life—Colorado. 3. Colorado—History—19th century. I. Title.

HQ145.C6W66 2005

306.74'2'0978809034—dc22

2004021719

Cover photo courtesy
The Old Homestead Museum
Cripple Creek, Colorado

Printed and bound in the United States of America by
Caxton Press
Caldwell, Idaho 83605
171781

TABLE OF CONTENTS

Illustrations

ACKNOWLEDGEMENTS

We learn from our history, and women were and are very much a part of it.

Women in history is a fascination I have held since early childhood. Weekend trips to the Rocky Mountains were filled with my mother's stories of Clear Creek Annie, Mollie Brown and Baby Doe Tabor. Through my mother's narratives, I formed a life-long love of Colorado history and particularly, the women. So, I decided to write a history of Colorado's neglected women.

Assembling the research, which in itself was skimpy, was a tedious task. I received a wealth of support. Once again, Denver University Professor Tom Noel steered me in the right direction. And again, I relied on historical societies across the state. Darrell Lindsey of Florence supplied corroborating information regarding Lillian Powers, and Linda Jones of Gilpin County generously shared her knowledge of Central City bordellos. Duane Smith, professor of history at Fort Lewis College in Durango, helped with research in the Durango area, and gave invaluable insight.

Special thanks go to a few people who believed in this project and gave freely of their time and advice. First on that list is my husband, Frank, who tolerated the many late nights of research and writing and helped to work out the research obstacles. My sister Stephanie stepped up to the plate when asked, editing the manuscript, assembling the index, and most importantly, becoming my support line. Maggie Stephens of the Fort Morgan Museum, a family friend, lent her skills in the phrasing and punctuation. And finally, to Wayne Cornell, my editor, who believed in this project from the beginning, and whose advice, suggestions, insight, and direction, kept the manuscript in focus, and perhaps more than any other, has shaped this work.

To all of you, a grateful thank you.

PRELUDE

———✦———

Historians have long recognized the achievements of men in the old West — the trappers, cowboys and gunfighters and the males who established the first businesses. The chroniclers however, for the most part, ignored the significant role played by the first businesswomen — members of the "world's oldest profession" — in the settling of the frontier. Only recently have the "delicate" subjects of women been written about. Over the years, a few works on the subject have been produced. Localized in nature, the writings usually focus on a particular region and the soiled doves of that area.

Prostitutes made their appearance in Colorado soon after the first mining claims were staked. "Our ladies of the tenderloin," as they were sometimes called in newspapers stories of the day, were an integral element of many communities well into the twentieth century. Some of the better known red light districts across Colorado were Aspen, Central City, Colorado City, Cripple Creek, Creede, Denver's Market Street, Durango, Florence, Georgetown, Lake City, Leadville, and Salida.

This book makes no pretense to be a definitive history of Colorado prostitution. It is rather an attempt to bring the stories of soiled doves from across Colorado together — to bring their lives, however triumphant or tragic, into historical perspective. It is hoped the portraits of these women will be both informative and entertaining.

Without notice they came, and without notice they disappeared, leaving little evidence they were ever here. A plot in a cemetery or an occasional mention in the local paper seems to be the only memorials to frontier prostitutes. But they left their mark in the form of history, perhaps a bit dramatic or even provocative, yet a history worth recounting.

Women are as much a part of American history as their male counterparts. It is time the history of women, in all venues and aspects, be told for all that they were and are.

INTRODUCTION

"I went into the sporting life for business reasons and for no other. It was a way for a woman in those days to make money and I made it." — Mattie Silks

With the discovery of gold in 1858, the population of Colorado's Rocky Mountain region exploded. On the heels of greenhorns and tenderfeet, eager to strike it rich, came the women, and usually for the same reasons. And many of the early female arrivals were "ladies of the evening."

The prostitutes of the early American West and Colorado were, by and large, a group of strong willed and tough women. The "soiled doves" catered to the young and lonely men, and (for the most part) they were welcomed. Prostitutes were in wide demand, even respected to a point. Theirs was the only female touch in cold, dirty mining camps or hot, dusty, lonely prairie encampments. They brought a sort of refinement, as only women can, along with conversation, companionship, and, oh yes, sex.

Westward migration, with all its opportunities and promise, posed an entirely new set of circumstances for most women. Far from the civilized cities of the East, women found themselves without luxuries and conveniences. They learned to adapt to the land and became self-sufficient, and none more so than the prostitute.

Many prostitutes did quite well in the booming days of Colorado's mining era. With very few women in the mining camps, the soiled doves were a welcome form of female companionship in every sense of the word.

Of course this all changed with a slow, yet building crusade of morality. The reformers believed they were working for a higher authority, and called for an end to prostitution. But their demands weren't accepted quickly by many males in the developing communities.

Many of Colorado's demimonde regarded their profession as an economic opportunity. The majority of these women came from middle class families in the East, or were fallen women who were already in the business before coming West.

And we must not forget the women who entered the profession because of some sad, dark past, and therefore felt they had no other choice. In their minds a loss of virtue meant a loss of self respect.

By the late nineteenth century, social changes were taking place. The carefree, wild and wicked ways of Colorado's early frontier became a thing of the past. Families built communities and communities built respect.

Yet, before all of this change, there were the women who offered their own unique services in a new and developing land we now call Colorado. Their stories are every bit as dramatic as the men who mined, legislated, built roads and then railroads, fought, and otherwise developed the towns and cities that became the foundation of the state.

Historical accounts of "our ladies" can be found in newspaper archives, particularly obituaries and criminal cases. Other sources include census records, cemetery records, and a few business directories. However, a majority of prostitutes lived in shades of gray. By moving from town to town and by changing their names and inventing past lives, the identities of these women constantly evolved. Today it is often difficult to separate historical truth and folklore.

The Victorian terms used in newspapers and other writings of the period are used in this work. References to soiled doves, women of the underworld, courtesan, bagnio, demimonde, madam, mistress, and painted lady all describe the prostitute.

Common terms, such as parlor house, brothel and bordello, need little explanation. For the more colorful terms such as hog ranch, tenderloin, the line, crib and hurdy-gurdy, a full description is given in Chapter One.

A curious explanation for one term seldom used in this work, is "hooker." The term evidently dates back to the 1860s, and became quite popular during the Civil War. Union General Joseph Hooker took an unconventional approach regarding prostitutes who frequented the military camps.

General Hooker sensed the need, or at least the desire, of his men in this regard. In an effort to boost the moral, General Hooker simply looked the other way. So it was that men under his command came to call the ladies in question, "hookers," an endearment obviously in honor of their leader.

In recent years, many works have been published on the social aspects of prostitution. These works tend to focus on the analysis of reasons, motives, mind sets, causes, actions and reactions of prostitutes as a whole, rather than the individual and her circumstances. The psychologist approach seems unending, and — well — deep. This book takes a different tack, centering around the lives of the prostitutes. I have focused on the individual woman's character, experiences and contribution to frontier society, however great or small each may have been.

History and folklore are wrestled apart in an effort to focus on the prostitute as a member of true historical frontier society, rather than a mere footnote in the many accounts of the Wild, Wild West.

Our Ladies of the Tenderloin
COLORADO'S LEGENDS IN LACE

The West. The term brings to mind images of wide open spaces, new beginnings and opportunities, all wild and colorful. There were shoot-outs, fast guns. pioneers, Indians, soldiers, gamblers, millionaires, buffalo hunters, railroad tycoons . . . and women.

Into the mix of Colorado's frontier came Pearl DeVere, Lillis Lovell, Marie Contessant and Cock-eyed Liz, along with Sallie Purple, Ella Wellington, Lizzie Preston and Mattie Silks. There was the beautiful Jennie Rogers, who built a house of mirrors, scandalized by rumors of blackmail and murder. These women were part of the Tenderloin District and just about every Colorado town had one.

They were Colorado's legends in lace.

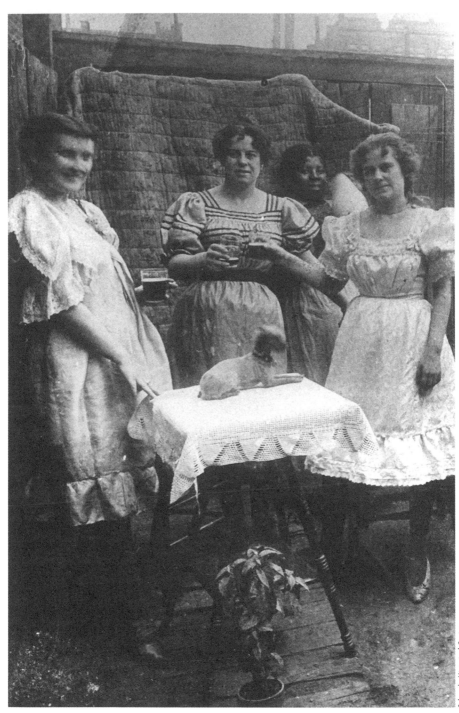

ONE

First came the miners to work in the mine.
Then came the ladies who worked on the line.

Parlor House Particulars

Some people claimed Myers Avenue was the liveliest street in the West. A popular song of the period, *There'll be a Hot Time in the Old Town Tonight*, is said to have originated on Myers Avenue in the "World's Greatest Gold Camp" of Cripple Creek, Colorado. And it fit! For Myers Avenue was one of the largest and most boisterous streets of ill repute in all of the West, and the site of a legendary Red Light District.

On April 25, 1896, during a heated moment at the *Central Dance Hall*, one of the girls known as Jennie, while fighting with a customer, fell against the coal burning stove which toppled over, igniting the dance hall and soon, much of Cripple Creek. The town rebuilt, this time with brick, yet the tenderloin district along Myers Avenue remained largely built of wood.

Our Ladies of the Tenderloin proved to have a sense of humor when they adopted poodles as their pets. Although the shaving is a mystery, it was an obvious thumb of the nose to high society women who owned poodles as status symbols.

Myers Avenue was located one block south of the main street, Bennett Avenue and ran from approximately Fifth Street, east to the Poverty Gulch area.

After the 1896 fire, one establishment on the "row" became known throughout the West. The April 30, 1896 edition of the *Cripple Creek Times* reported: "The madame turned from her $2,000.00 loss of Saturday, placed an order for lumber, and was back in business on Tuesday."

The "business" was called the *Old Homestead,* and became legendary for its service, its clientele and its famous madams. Located at 353 Myers Avenue, the *madame* mentioned in the news article is presumably Hazel Vernon, the first madam of Cripple Creek. Her new parlor house was quite extravagant for the times. Tongues wagged at the amount of money Hazel spent to make her house of ill repute the finest in all Colorado. And for a time, it was. Lavish decorations, from furniture to lace curtains, adorned the parlor area and the rooms upstairs. Large fireplaces as well as coal stoves heated the house on cold Cripple Creek nights. Electric lights kept the house alive during gay parties for rich clientele. Running water eased the maintenance and improved the cleanliness of the establishment, not to mention the women. The *Old Homestead* would become a Colorado legend because of another famous madam who later would own the establishment, Pearl DeVere.

⚐ THE TERM "RED LIGHT DISTRICT" is derived from the railroad customers who frequented the Line — the section of town where houses of prostitution were located. Railroad workers, seeking a bit of "relaxation" during stop-overs, would oftentimes take their red signal lanterns with them, placing them in front of the particular dwelling of pleasure. Thus, the term Red Light District was born. It also is possible the catch phrase, "the wrong side of the tracks," originates from the same connotation.

Most red light districts were on the lower or less desirable side of town. In many cases, towns expanded away from the railroad lines to avoid the noise and the pollution. In this way, the red light district became a distinct area, separated from the rest of the community. And nearly every town had one.

Durango, Colorado was the exception. That southwestern mountain town boomed in 1880 to provide not one, but *two* red light districts! The earlier of the two inhabited the railroad area, while the second occupied the west side of a portion of Main Avenue.

Boulder's red light district was located on Water Street, a block south of the Colorado & Southern railroad tracks, the vicinity of today's Boulder Public Library. The district, located on 11th Street, ran near the Boulder Creek. Marietta

Kingsley ran a very popular parlor house on nearby Walnut Street. From the 1880s until the early 1900s, the Boulder newspapers were spiced with stories of Madam Kingsley and her *White House* of ill-repute. Fights would break out, raids were a regular occurrence, and even murder happened in Kingsley's domain.

A colorful character, Kingsley was rarely seen without her two small pug dogs. During the flood of 1894, Kingsley was rescued from the rushing waters by a Doctor Jay. Emerging soaking wet, she had managed to hang on to both dogs.

Aspen prostitutes operated on Durant Street, also near the railroad tracks, between Hunter and Spring Streets, the "other side of the tracks" in that community. The popular bordellos of Breckenridge, *The Blue Goose* and *Minnie's House*, were also located near the railroad depot. In Telluride, Colorado Avenue was the dividing line. The social elite were never seen on the south side of the street — or they at least tried to avoid being recognized in that area.

In Ouray, the Vanoli brothers ran an unusual boarding house. They built their famous *220 Dance House* and *Roma Saloon* shortly after their arrival from Italy, in 1884. The upstairs of the 220 Dance House contained the rooms of hired girls practicing their trade. The Vanoli business was such a success in Ouray, the brothers opened another dance hall in Telluride, managed by Dominck Vanoli's son, Tony. Other bordellos in Ouray included *The Monte Carlo, The Clipper, Bon Ton*, and *The Morning Star*, all located on Second Street, between 7th and 8th streets.

In Central City, the red light district originally in the heart of the town and known as the "Richest Square Mile on Earth," was moved to the southern outskirts in 1868. The hillside on the south end of Pine Street near the train depot is a very small area where once, up to six frame houses served as bordellos, perhaps the most compact district in all of Colorado. Looking at the hillside today, where only a few native rock foundations can be seen, it is hard to imagine frame houses built into the hillside and then butted next to each other length-wise. Yet, Central City's Pine Street was an active area of town.

Parlor houses were run by and, more often than not, owned by women, who were typically known as madams. These houses were the finest forms of the prostitution trade. The number of women ranged from six to twenty, depending on the size of the house and the madam's business acumen. The madams provided the girls, who ranged from age fifteen to thirty, with room and board in exchange for a percentage of their earnings. Again, depending on the size of the establishment, the parlor house would have servants or, in some cases, the girls were expected to help out with such chores as cleaning and cooking.

Cleanliness was a matter of opinion in the red light district, in the days before local and state health officials regulated the houses. As a matter of choice, long before medical regulation, parlor house madams generally had strict rules on cleanliness. Their image, and their high profile clientele, demanded it. Linens were changed between customers, the girls washed between customers, and often quite discreetly, checked their paying guests.

The parlor house girls were required to look and dress their best during the entertaining hours, reflecting the image of the house and the madam. Most of the girls had little spending money and were encouraged to charge their purchases to the madam's accounts at local stores. The madam, in turn, depending on her individual character, charged each girl interest on her purchases.

The required clothing varied, depending on the type of house, the madam, and the environment. For instance, Denver's brides of the multitude generally wore fine silks in the latest fashion. Crib girls often wore cotton or linen night dresses, as did many soiled doves of the mountain mining camps.

One prostitute, known only as LaVerne, worked for years with madam Laura Evans during Laura's years in Denver.[1] LaVerne commented during an interview about the character and manners expected of the soiled doves in a parlor house:

> Miss Laura never wanted us girls to talk loud, and we were always taught to watch our language. We parlor house girls never used four-letter words. Miss Laura said 'You can still be a lady and be in the district.' Miss Laura would tell us never to come in the parlor with a gingham dress on — that's what a man sees all day at home.

Social standards existed within the world of prostitution. There was a major social difference between the elegant parlor house and the local brothel. To the customers, there was a significant difference as well: the cost of such services.

To the women of the red light districts, the brothel was a social step below the parlor house. Brothel madams tended to be more lax with regard to the girls they employed, both in appearance and age. The terms of employment were often more rigid with less freedom offered and a higher percentage taken. Often the customer traffic was higher in a brothel, and therefore, the girls worked harder and longer.

The difference between the dance hall and the common saloon could oftentimes be a fine line. The dance hall, designed as a type of variety show, employed women to dance and sing for the male clientele, as well as secure whatever business they could on the side. This was a coy way of eliciting illegal business. The female dancers were known throughout the West as "hurdy-gurdy girls." Dance hall girls or hurdy-gurdy girls who doubled as prostitutes were detested by the parlor house girls.

The brass check or coin came into being as a medium of exchange within the world of the parlor houses. Designed as a standard token, the customer knew what he was charged for when receiving the tokens, usually in turn for his silver dollars. The tokens were then given to the prostitute upon receipt of her services. At the end of business, usually in the early morning hours, the tokens would be accounted for by the madam.

In the case of the dance hall or saloon, a customer was given the favor of a free dance, followed by a drink at the bar with his companion. In exchange for his fifty cent piece, he received a drink and a brass token, which allowed him the chance to negotiate for further favors from the girl, who pocketed the brass token for later accounting.

Over time, many writers and in particular, the western movie explosion from the 1940s through the 1960s, depicted the saloon girls as voluptuous women with sing song voices. In reality, the stage show, if there was one, consisted of an average of three girls who sang and danced a tune or two to the best of their abilities. This was only an enticement for the men to buy more drinks for themselves and for the ladies who eventually mingled with them. This was the real stage for the women of the dance halls and saloons. Rooms were reserved on the upper floor in most cases, for the development of "further income" to the proprietor.

Anne Gibbon did not fling her elephantine limbs high enough to dodge the bullets in the dance hall in Silver Cliff. — The Rocky Mountain News, December 7, 1878

Following the Civil War, many black women, helpless in the "New South," turned to prostitution. It is said these women exchanged one form of slavery for another. However, those who made their way to Colorado found themselves welcomed, for the most part, into the soiled dove sisterhood.

One such woman was the enterprising madam Molly Gordon, who broke many barriers in Boulder's tenderloin district. Molly was one of the few black madams in Colorado. She owned a fashionable bordello at 1034 Water Street in 1878, called *The Temple Venus*. Molly had a long time lover, but when the two went to

Denver Public Library

Cripple Creek's Myers Avenue looking north from the center of the city. Note the crib area as the parlor houses get smaller toward the end of the "line."

The famous *Old Homestead* parlor house on Cripple Creek's Myers Avenue, caused wonder, wagging tongues and weariness for the borders.

Author's collection

Carrie Nation, on behalf of the Women's Temperance Union, wielded her axe as well as her tongue in many a Colorado mining town.

On Denver's infamous Market Street, this photo shows the girls of the tenderloin end, as they lurk for customers.

Boulder's city officials to obtain a license for marriage, they were denied. Apparently, it was against the law for blacks and whites to wed in holy matrimony. Molly's long-time love was a white man. So the two simply lived together happily in Molly's less than holy temple.

❧ LEADVILLE'S LADIES OF THE TENDERLOIN resided on the lower end of town, just off the main street of commerce, Harrison Avenue. Within a two- to three-block section of State Street, the fancy parlor houses dwelt among the dance halls and cribs. Leadville was a mining boom town turned metropolis and money flowed freely. While most girls on the row had plenty of business, dance hall and crib girls still envied the girls of the parlor houses, with their fancy clothes and jewelry. These women often vied for the same clientele. Mean, vicious and often deadly fights ensued. It was only a matter of time before envy spilled over to jealousy and jealousy into rivalry, the likes of which only female spite can produce. The cat fights between the girls on the line generally involved shoving, biting, hitting and kicking. Amusing at times, perhaps, but never pleasant.

Such an incident occurred in Cripple Creek's red light district area. One of the more colorful ladies of the tenderloin was Mollie, a part-time crib girl and part-time laundress. Mollie had a passion for bull dogs and raised puppies for sale. One day a drunken miner stole one of the puppies and gave it as payment to another soiled dove along the row. As soon as Mollie found out, she went to collect her puppy. The confrontation turned into a brawl, with Mollie knocking the woman down in the mud. When the city's law enforcement arrived, Mollie wasn't finished and knocked two of policemen into the mud as well! Eventually, Mollie was subdued by more officers and hauled off to jail in the paddy wagon.

The competition heated up in Durango following the Silver Panic of 1893. When the mines shut down in the surrounding towns, the brides of the multitude boarded trains bound for Durango. The Durango depot would be crowded with men every Saturday afternoon to catch a glimpse of the new "entertainment." The girls of Durango's red light district were on hand as well — not to greet the new arrivals so much as to eye the competition. For months, the arrivals seemed endless. From Telluride and Creede, Leadville and Glenwood Springs, and even Denver, the women arrived for work and fortune in Durango. When the prostitutes of Silverton arrived, the men cheered at their good fortune!

In general, local newspapers said very little about prostitution. While an obvious attraction and necessity in most communities, the Victorian attitude seemed to be to look the other way. As the community jelled, and respectability in the form of family, churches, and schools grew, more newspaper editors took a reformist attitude.

Mollie May, Leadville's most famous madam, got into a little tiff with another soiled dove. What made this incident interesting is that the local paper seemed to enjoy reporting the events. In the summer of 1882, Mollie went to the police and swore out a complaint against Annie Layton for stealing a dress. In retaliation, Annie had a warrant drawn up against Mollie for running a house of prostitution. Mollie answered the summons by stating Annie was a "member of said house." The paper then editorialized, "It is likely these charges will be withdrawn, as both parties would be almost unable to prove their charges without incriminating themselves." In the next issue, the paper reported that all charges had been dropped.

Evidently, headlines do make a difference.

"Aunt Jane," as she was called, was an older black woman who plied her trade on Myers Avenue. *The Cripple Creek Times* reported:

> "Aunt Jane," the aged colored lady, well-known to the police here, got in bad again. She was found guilty in police court yesterday of drunkenness and disorderly conduct and was fined $1.00 and costs. She will be permitted to work out her fine in cleaning up the jail. At this she is said to be first class and when "Auntie" gets through her jobs as vale de chambers at the city bastille the place is expected to look like the 'Gold Dust Twins' had taken a hand in the affair.

In the larger towns, Denver in particular, newspaper reporters reveled in writing about the torrid incidents in the bordellos and saloons. Denver's many saloons had graduated to higher standards, that is, in clientele and prices. On Blake Street, they were known as variety halls and employed the same scantily clad women who danced, served drinks and provided various services "on the side." Establishments such as the *Cricket* and the *Progressive Club* lined both sides of Blake Street.

Perhaps the most famous was Ed Chase's *Palace Theatre*, which was later owned by Bat Masterson for a short time. Curtained boxes adorned the walls on the second and third floor levels, providing excellent views of the stage below. The *Palace* could hold 750, with lines of customers waiting to be admitted often stretching down the street. A full menu was available, complete with a midnight buffet, as well as a fully stocked bar, and of course, rooms available upstairs. The occasional murder still occurred, as did the more often love affairs, never ending deceit and constant thievery.

In Durango, the *Phoenix Variety Theatre* was a showplace. The opulent main floor, lined with thick Victorian rugs and rich furniture, shimmered in the warm glow of the many chandeliers hanging from the high ceiling. Gentlemen clients mingled and relaxed with drinks and pretty female servers. The rich velvet draped theatre upstairs ran a mix of comedy, drama, musicals, and female dancing performances to sell-out crowds. But the main attraction was upstairs through a back staircase where small rooms provided privacy. It was here that before, during, and after the theatre performance one floor below, the girls of the Phoenix performed for a private audience.

The Line is another term meant to distinguish the bawdy area of town. As small towns or mining camps grew into communities, the red light district was systematically moved away from town. In Aspen, the line was moved against a mountainside, in Central City it was crammed against a hillside at the end of a tiny street. In Salida, it was moved near the noisy railroad line, and in Telluride, the line was moved to the near-edge of the San Miguel River. Thus, *the line* became a wholesale term for the prostitute's area of business. A common term we use today dates from this time: "the end of the line." Another enduring term, *the Tenderloin*, comes from the East Coast. Segregation of prostitutes began in New York City in the 1830s. The original section of town where the prostitutes were forced to relocate was an area near the slaughter houses and meat markets. With that, the common term "tenderloin" took on a whole new meaning.

At the end of the line were the cribs. These one-room dwellings were the lowest form of tenderloin social order. Cripple Creek's crib section was typical of most Colorado mining towns. The tenderloin district of Myers Avenue began at Fifth Street with the *Old Homestead* parlor house, and graduated east to the crib area, near Poverty Gulch and the seamy side of town. This sordid area was the typical location in most Colorado towns for the cribs. Pine shacks lined the gulch for nearly a half a mile in Cripple Creek's lower section, with a few still visible today.

Most cribs in Colorado's red light districts were one-room wooden structures containing a stove, a chair and, of course, a bed. A few of the cribs had windows which the women used for advertising. Often cribs were cold, dark and dirty. Newspaper accounts described them as "insect haunted walls," or "smoke filled, filthy and damp." For a good portion of the demimonde, it was a deplorable existence. It was not just a working room for the soiled dove, this was her home! The women of the cribs were of various races and often past their prime years. Many were drug addicts or alcoholics.

Such was the case of Leo the Lion. Madam Leo, as she was commonly known, was an aged prostitute eking out a sad living in a crib on Cripple Creek's Myers Avenue. Ravaged by alcohol, the woman became a pathetic figure on the row. In one incident recounted in the Cripple Creek newspapers, a drunken Leo the Lion waltzed out of her crib in broad daylight, stark naked, and proclaimed: "I am the queen of the row." Caring miners returned her to her crib to sleep off her condition. She was not arrested. It seems the Cripple Creek law enforcement could be compassionate. It was Leo the Lion who enticed a young reporter of *Collier's Magazine* in an interview, that caused him to write his blazing article on Cripple Creek in 1914. The article was taken to heart by the city fathers of Cripple Creek, causing a bit of a ruckus for a time. Evidently, Leo the Lion gave her interview in such a crude fashion, the young reporter was taken aback. From her crib window, she first enticed the gentleman with sexual favors and then, upon learning who he was, she proceeded to voice her own opinions about the town. As the reporter took his leave, Leo the Lion was supposed to have said: ". . . send some nice boys by sometime." Sounds a bit like Mae West.

Thus, as prostitution grew, a sense of soiled dove social class status began to emerge. The women of the cribs in tenderloin sections across Colorado were the working masses of prostitution, yet scorned by the female society as a whole.

Sweet Betsy From Pike

Prostitution on the Plains of Colorado, scarce as it was, did exist. Following the Civil War, westward migration intensified, creating a need for military protection along the new frontier. In Colorado, forts were built and army personnel grew ever more prevalent on the plains. For soldiers stationed there, isolation and a lack of social recreation in the wind-blown, bleak new wilderness led to boredom and depression. With the arrival of the occasional prostitute, followed later by wagons and caravans of women, human sexuality could no longer be denied and was nearly uncontrollable, as the army, for the most part, looked the other way; it was good for morale, overall. The obvious change in morale led to the relaxed conditions on and off base, at least for a time.

Thus, prostitution on the eastern plains existed primarily near forts and commerce areas along the westward trails through Colorado. Later the railroads, and communities were built, which included the soiled doves. In Pueblo, there was Madam Mabel Miller, and Trinidad had S. Cunningham and May Phelps.

While most prostitutes set up camp near the military forts or early frontier towns, a few followed or even joined the cavalry on their patrols or marches. One such woman was Calamity Jane. Martha Jane Canary has always eluded the historian. Her life and exploits are legendary, but mixed with truth and conjecture. Her own autobiography is the basis for much of the frustration.

We do know from historical records Jane was once a "boarder," of "Madam Moustache," a famed madam of Wyoming and Montana. She worked in Cheyenne and other towns along the the Union Pacific Railroad line. By 1889, Calamity Jane was residing in quarters at a new community near the Fort Collins military fort in northern Colorado. Here, her services were strictly of a human nature. For several months, Calamity Jane provided her "female companionship" to soldiers for a price. It is said she later performed the same duties for the soldiers near La Junta, probably Fort Lyon.[2] She was also known to have been working at a so-called "hotel" in Boulder in 1893.

Many military prostitutes followed a similar routine. The accommodations used by these women acquired an interesting name. Often, isolated army forts put out bids for their ranching neighbors to provide beef for the soldiers. Pork was harder to obtain, as most early ranchers raised cattle. Diet seems to have been important to the military even then, and so hog ranches were built at or near the forts.

A long building with several entries would serve as the quarters or bunk house for the men who tended the hogs. In time, as small caravans of prostitutes appeared routinely at the military posts, they were allowed to share a separate portion of the bunk house. Thus, a new category of the prostitution hierarchy emerged in the West: the "hog ranch."

In many prostitution social circles, the hog ranches were almost worse than the cribs. Denver's Market Street madam, Lizzie Preston, began her illustrious career at a hog ranch. It is said Ella Watson, better known in history as "Cattle Kate," once worked for Lizzie on Denver's Market Street. The two had a lot in common and later, Cattle Kate went to Stillwater, Wyoming where she established a hog ranch of her own, with partner Jim Averill. The two would meet their fate by hanging during the infamous Johnson County War.

In 1898, a hog ranch operation existed on the outskirts of Denver near the railroad tracks, according to a newspaper's articles and police reports of the day. Sarah

Gillis and her daughter Alice, operated the hog ranch as well as a gang of sorts who stole various items from the railroad. Nevertheless, prostitution was a mainstay of the hog ranch operation. In 1899, detective Sam Howe cracked the case, and Sarah and her daughter Alice were arrested. Both were convicted of robbery and sent to prison. However, the story of the Gillis women does not end here. In 1892, daughter Alice, released from prison, was soon arrested again. The local newspapers followed the story closely, as Alice was pregnant and about to give birth to the first child born in the city jail!

It was about 4:30 a.m. when Jailer Hughley Smith heard a slight disturbance that made him enter (the) jail just as Alice became a mother. Every attention was given the tiny little stranger fresh from No Man's Land, but it lived only a few moments. The woman's presence in the jail was due to a disturbance between herself and the infant's father. Of course the man was brutally drunk and acted like a brute when he dealt her the cowardly blow. He kicked her and beat her. It was a tiny little infant, and just opened its eyes long enough to see the light of the world. That was all. Something in the ex-queen of the hog ranch, though she was, responded to a touch of nature and seeing that he might die, asked to have him baptized. It was a solemn moment, and the ceremony was barely over before the tiny offspring of the "queen of the hog ranch" closed its tender little eyes, gave one gasp and died.[3]

In alley ways, in the back of lower class bordellos, and in some cribs, were the opium dens. While a part of the tenderloin district, primarily by location only, the opium dens were a separate operation. Public sentiment regarding these incense invested dens was so strong that most towns shut them down or forced them out. Narcotic use, then as now, was almost impossible to stop completely, and the opium dens were no exception. They simply went underground to other areas of the city.

Our ladies of the tenderloin contributed to the local economy, regardless of the particular locale. Working men spent their hard earned money on recreation . . . with the lady of their choice. She, in turn, spent her money on local purchases of her choice. Money spent locally was returned locally and everyone prospered.

By the mid nineteenth century, prostitution was a multi-million dollar business in the United States. This fact was not lost on the officials of Colorado towns, cities and mining camps. In many cases, such as Silverton, a town's operating cap-

ital came almost entirely from license fees, permits, and fines levied against prostitutes and gambling establishments.[4]

Business fees and fines soon followed and if either weren't paid, the law would
step in. There was a fine line between exercising compliance and outright control.
In a remote town like Silverton, control was in the hands of corrupt lawmen and
politicians. Often the lawmen would raise fines or fees without authorization and
pocket the difference collected. It wasn't a practice without appreciation, however, for the lawmen who then patrolled Blair Street would often look the other way
if "certain" businesses were bending the law a bit. The system worked for a time
and everyone made money, from the city treasury to the barkeep. In Silverton's
case, famed lawman Bat Masterson eventually was called in to tame the corrup-
tion, with little success. This practice was soon followed in some form in most
Colorado communities.

Each madam was taxed anywhere from ten to twenty dollars a month, depending on the size of her establishment, and of course, based on individual city or
county taxation laws. Each girl was then taxed from two to eight dollars per month
in the same fashion.

Medical requirements also became law and fairly routine. On average, each
girl made a monthly visit to a local doctor who generally pronounced her clean
and healthy. For his services, the doctor received an average of two dollars per
"patient." In some communities, he even received a kickback from the city, in an
effort to keep the "sinful revenue" flowing in a "clean" manner. Doctors also treated sexual diseases. The treatments were often painful and occasionally included
operations. Various forms of venereal disease occurred. Some were treatable, some
were not. Once afflicted with the incurable disease, the soiled dove was "burned,"
a general term for her affliction. Abortions were rare but did indeed exist, using
drugs that usually caused a long, riveting and painful ordeal.

PROHIBITION & REFORMATION

As mining camps became towns, and towns became cities, a natural progres-
sion emerged: civilization, in the form of women, children and family. Thus a
transformation occurred from the former working camp or town atmosphere, to a
community resplendent with schools, churches, and social affairs. It was an atmosphere that only women could achieve.

One woman traveling west in 1869 stopped in Julesburg. In her diary, she
wrote:

The women were worse than the men and I did not meet more than two of my own sex while I was there who made the most distant claims to even common decency or self respect.[5]

Saloons, dance halls and, prostitutes were the antithesis of Victorian purism. Society women wanted what they had left behind, churches and schools: symbols of society. They wanted comfort and security. Saloons and prostitutes were not only a deterrent to their Victorian ideal, they were a threat to their own womanhood.

Women's social organizations and Christian movements, such as the *Women's Christian Temperance Union*, promoted, crusaded, and rallied for the removal of drinking establishments, gambling halls, and especially houses of ill repute. It was the general opinion of these groups that the bordellos in particular were a threat to the overall morality of the citizens. Reformers in Denver, in 1871, urged and campaigned for high fees to be imposed on the establishments housing prostitution. The campaign eventually died for lack of interest.[6]

Most communities throughout the state adopted an "out of sight, out of mind" strategy regarding prostitution. While establishments of ill repute were allowed in the community, they were often restricted to one particular section of the town. This was usually classified as the "lower side," "edge," or "end" of town – usually one street.[7]

In Silverton, an ordinance in 1879 was passed, making it unlawful for saloons or all-night establishments, such as bordellos, to allow disorderly conduct, loud noise (including music) or employment of prostitutes.[8] The reformers further demanded closure of these sin-full establishments on the Sabbath. The men of Silverton loudly protested this notion. Sunday was the only day these working men had off. It was a day to catch up on chores, and maybe even relax and have some time to enjoy "leisure" activities.

When the city council of Pueblo first passed an ordinance confining and fining prostitution and prostitutes, the Pueblo Chieftain of January 14, 1875, ran this editorial:

. . . our city fathers have suddenly awakened to the fact that lewd women are to be found in Pueblo. The effect of prohibitory legislation upon these things is simply to make the carrying on of them rather more secret, and hence less under the

control of the police. We must conclude then that the ordinance is passed for the purpose of revenue.

Public apathy and limited law enforcement made reform attempts unsuccessful.

By 1874, the women of the West were becoming a sizable force for social change. Momentum for their cause hit a new level when the *Women's Christian Temperance Union* began a national crusade against sins of vice. Carrie Nation, famous spokesperson for the group, caused damage to saloons across the West, with her ax-wielding ways and righteous speeches. In the end, she probably did more harm than good for her cause.

For instance, in Colorado, when Carrie Nation came to Cripple Creek, she may not have swung her ax, but she did as much damage, as her words were plastered on the front pages of newspapers everywhere: "Cripple Creek is a foul cesspool."

Nation further stated the town, and Myers Avenue in particular, was, ". . . the wicked city of the entire nation." Followers of such headlines soon caught on. Every city Carrie Nation visited was given the same title.

Women's clubs in the East, indeed became a vehicle for social change. With no particular aim in the beginning, by the 1880s, women were demanding focus on the family, religion, and social structure. The movement spread westward, and in 1896, the righteous women of the Cripple Creek Mining District, were the first in Colorado to form their own Women's Club. In Victor, a member of the Women's Club wrote to the local newspaper of her observations of the Red Light District:

At the present Victor is a flourishing city of over ten thousand, the second largest city in the C.C. District. Due to the large number of men coming to the District in search of employment, the moral situation is bad. Victor has five flourishing churches . . . the saloons are supposed to be closed on Sunday but I hear that they are run on the open back door policy a part of the time. There is what is called the hottest burlesque theater of the West, the Union Theater, on 3rd St. Hardly a night passes without a serious brawl or shooting — but I understand (being a lady and a member of the Club, I cannot speak of first hand experience,) a girl known as Cleo the Egyptian Belly Dancer was run out of town, as her act was so indecent as to shock the hardened men who compose the audience of this

famous theater. There are a number of brothels and dance halls, and it is indeed
a pity to see so many young women and girls make their living in this way. The
ladies of the Club have talked to them and sent some of them home to their moth-
ers. Others have been sent to a house of correction where they will be taught to
be good women.

Gradually, the movement spread across Colorado. Within ten years of the Colorado gold rush of 1859, mining camps were communities, and women were working for social change. The calico dressed women took it upon themselves to change the very existence of social habitats their men folk established and enjoyed.

Their ideas did have some merit, but their men were in no way ready for social change in Colorado. In fact, men were so angered by the attacks against their beloved saloons, they would actually dump the beer kegs in front of the saloon, creating a muddy pool of slop, in an effort to thwart the female reformers from entering the establishment.

Righteous and pious men of the clergy almost uniformly condemned the soiled doves as shameless and hopeless. These women were considered products of the devil, with no hope of salvation. So much for the Bible passage, "Judge not, lest Ye be judged." Yet, not all men of the cloth were as judgmental.

With the death of Fanny Chambers, a popular prostitute of Aspen, her funeral was paid for by the girls of the row. The preacher included in his sermon, "Let he who is without sin cast the first stone . . ." Yet, the local paper reported the event with much disdain.[9]

That is not to say that men did not admire or even respect their women folk. "Women are the salt of the earth . . . as long as they stay home." One editor published his views in the local paper in prayer form: ". . . the very notion of female reformers is abhorrent . . . from the stockings and the bloomers . . . we get strong-minded she-males generally, Good Lord, deliver us."[10]

For all the determination these women possessed, the Women's Club concept lacked organization and focus. Their loosely-based social reform platform centered on gambling and prostitution. For the most part, the town council, in concert with most of the citizens, were not about to accept the social change (or lose the revenue) these women advocated. Unsure how to handle the dilemma, one Durango city councilman said, "Well boys, grass would be growing on Main Street if it weren't . . . for the miners spending their money."

❧ With heavy sighs all through Colorado's red light districts, the ladies of the tenderloin persevered.

The handful of reformers had their work cut out for them. The effect of temperance lectures by and large was nonexistent. The lectures, particularly when headlined by a national name, did draw large crowds. Because saloons were often the largest accommodations in town, the lectures would be held there, with all evidence of drink hidden or removed, of course. In reality, the reform movement was actually sensationalized by the fanatics who made national headlines, such as Carrie Nation and Susan B. Anthony. While these women wielded their wrath along with their axes in towns such as Lake City, Leadville, Cripple Creek, and Denver, most reform actions were small in citizen numbers across Colorado.

From farmers and ranchers, to businessmen and miners, men enjoyed hearing the speaker tell of his or her sinful past from drunkenness to adultery, all in a thunderous righteous tone. For the men in the audience, the lectures were a comedy based on sinful actions, and often better than any theater performance. Not only did men not take the reformers seriously, but in some instances, they even took great offense.

Case in point: Cripple Creek, Colorado. When the famous author of the day, Julian Street of *Collier's Magazine*, arrived in Cripple Creek, in 1914, Street wrote of a dirty dilapidated Cripple Creek, full of worn out houses and worn out women. He went on to describe old women staggering out of "box-stalls" or peering at him shamefully through a single dingy window. Street had wandered into Myers Avenue, the tenderloin of the Cripple Creek District. The citizens of Cripple Creek were outraged at such a callous, one sided attack on their town. The city fathers voiced their outrage by changing the name of Myers Avenue to Julian Street, soon after the national article was published.[11]

"The Dance Hall Must Move!"

That was the headline of the Victor Record of December 31, 1900. The paper related the minutes of the city council and their decision, unanimously, to close down the *Red Light* dance hall at the corner of Victor Avenue and First Street. According to the article, the attorney presenting the petition, who was not named by the paper, ". . . made quite an eloquent argument against vice and portrayed to the aldermen a picture of children passing by the hall on their way to and from the Victor high school." The proprietor was told he had fifteen days to vacate the premises.

The primary result of this reform movement was a chain reaction eventually resulting in cultural and social change. In early frontier towns and mining camps, men outnumbered women as much as six to one. In time, wives, daughters, and various female family members arrived on the scene changing the odds and the social tenor of the communities.

Yet, our ladies of the tenderloin did not give up without a fight.

Denver's city council passed an outrageous ordinance requiring all courtesans to wear yellow ribbons upon their clothing, thereby denoting their profession. In the ingenious thought process of the city council, the yellow badges would allow the "other" women to avoid the "underworld" class of women in public. True to form, these gutsy ladies of the tenderloin rebelled in a bold public way.

The very next day, following passage of the ordinance, the ladies of Denver's Market Street emerged from their respective bordellos, obliging the city council quite handsomely indeed. Led by Denver's "Queens of the Row," Jennie Rogers and Mattie Silks, the women walked down Fifteenth Street, resplendent in their dresses, shoes, stockings, hair ribbons, parasols and purses — all in a lovely shade of yellow.

The women made their point and the city ordinances faded away. For a time.

End Notes: Chapter One

1   Mazzulla files, CHS.
2   Otero, *My Life on the Frontier.*
3   The *Colorado Sun*, April 8, 1892, and the Sam Howe scrapbooks.
4   Silverton Town Hall City Records Book 1, Ordinance Book A.
5   Miller, *Shady Ladies of the West* pg. 20
6   *The Rocky Mountain News*, September 10 and 17, 1871.
7   The town of Silverton is one exception. Notorious Blair Street is still in the middle of town.
8   West, *The Saloon on the Rocky Mountain Mining Frontier.* pg.139.
9   Aspen's *Rocky Mountain Sun*, August 23, 1884.
10 Reiter, *The Women.*
11 Myers Avenue has since been restored to its original name.

TWO

"I never took a girl into my house . . . who had no previous experience of life and men. That was a rule of mine . . . No innocent young girl was ever hired by me." — Laura Evans

Ladies of the Lamplight

Many nineteenth century Colorado soiled doves were true to the Victorian Age, providing their services with grace and charm. Other prostitutes were the embodiment of the carefree, lawless and often wild time that early Colorado also represented.

Somewhere in the middle were the average "Ladies of the Lamplight." These women conformed and adapted to the ways of the underworld, much as early Coloradans adapted from a Wild West lawless mentality, to a civilized body of community citizens who, by that time, welcomed law and order.

"Silver Queen of the Rockies" is how many historians describe Silverton, Colorado. Nestled in the San Juan Mountains, Silverton poured forth silver ore causing a massive population increase by 1874. Silverton's Blair Street was one of the more notorious streets of vice in the state. Among the forty some saloons and gambling halls, were the bordellos.

The beautiful Lillis Lovell made her way from the mining camp of Creede, to Denver's Market Street, where she became a successful madam.

In the early years of Silverton, prostitution was primarily confined to the dance halls along Blair and Greene Streets. Blair Street became the infamous mountain red light district around 1878. Most local historians use this date, due to the purchase of a "female boarding" house by Alice Morris. The sale was recorded in September of that year. The majority of the dance halls and bordellos were located between 11th and 13th Streets. *The Arlington* was a popular place in Silverton in 1883, when the famous gunslinger and ex-marshal Wyatt Earp spent time dealing cards there.

Blair Street business owners allegedly controlled the city politics and something had to be done about the "sinfulness" of the row. The city council brought in the famous lawman Bat Masterson to tame the town. As sheriff, Masterson did what he was hired to do, but never did close down Blair Street. Miners spent their pay on Blair Street and that meant a better economy for Silverton, even if the city council didn't like it. It was pure economics.

Actually it would seem the good citizens of Silverton were more concerned with the vice of gambling, than the prostitution. This *Silverton Democrat* editorial is typical of the time:

> *There are 27 saloons in this mining camp, nine of them in the block opposite the hotel. In one a man is yelling out the numbers of the 'Wheel of Fortune' in a noise that counter fits the music of a tin pan and stove lifter. At night the uproar is hideous. A loud piano in one den runs through three charming chords, drowning a vile squeaking fiddle from seven in the evening until sleep has mercifully closed one's ears. Farther down the block is heard the singing of a woman whose voice is much too good for the surroundings, for there are faro tables in all of these holes. The betting and drinking are pretty heavy when the miners are freshly paid up, and they revel in a beer at 15 cents a glass or two for a quarter, and get much foam and glass for the money.[1]*

Among the many houses of Blair Street was the Tremont, at 557 Blair Street. Owned and operated by Celeste Fattor and his wife Matilda, the establishment advertised ". . . eleven charming assistants." Matilda was a beloved character on the row. She was a large, jolly individual who always had a smile and a helping hand for anyone she came in contact with. Swedish by birth, she came to America about 1888, at the age of thirteen, where she first lived in Georgetown with her father. Matilda moved to Ouray at the age of eighteen, and later to Silverton. She married Celeste Fattor of Durango in 1905. The couple settled in Silverton, where everyone became their friends. In 1918, Matilda died in one of the upper rooms of the *Tremont Saloon*. A large woman, a special coffin was built from two regular coffins joined together. The majority of Silverton attended the simple service. Her body was then shipped to relatives in the East.

Cora Livingston's house was simply known as the *Big House,* and Stella Allison's place was also a popular attraction. Jane Bowen, also known as "Sage Hen," ran the notorious *Westminster* and *Palace* halls. Ludwig Vota held several properties on Blair Street which he leased to prostitutes, including "Jew" Fanny, Mayme Murphy, Kate Stair, and Annie James.

Ruby Reed made her living on Silverton's notorious Blair Street. She was favorably known among her kind to be honest and generous. Perhaps due to the loneliness of her occupation, she put a gun to her head early on the morning of October 11, 1897. She was nineteen years old.

Skip to My Lou My Darling

Girls will be girls, and sometimes the soiled doves just wanted to have fun. However, because they were the girls of the row, their escapades often made headlines. The *Rocky Mountain News* reported that Annie Griffin, Belle Jones, and Daisy Smith were in such a good mood they felt compelled to dance nude on a Larimer Street corner. The girls were arrested by embarrassed police for "naughty capers."

The *Leadville Chronicle* had a field day when Laura LeClair, a dance hall girl, got into a fight with Lillie Vane. Laura finally clobbered her foe with a billy club. Laura was arrested and eventually her case was dismissed.

According to the *Aspen Weekly Times*, Mary Murphy, a local prostitute who had had a bit too much to drink, chose to do a bit of "advertising" on the streets of Aspen. The police arrested Mary for parading naked in the street and hauled her off to jail. As she could not post the five dollar fine, she remained overnight in jail. Upon her release, the paper reported:

> Mary now is in her right mind, as well as in her ordinary wearing apparel, and is sorry that she looked upon the wine when it was red.

Madam Day and Susie Brown were the popular girls of Boulder's red light district. The two were bitter rivals for years. Their constant fighting occasionally led to violence including clubbing, gunfire, and arson. The *Boulder Daily Camera* reported such incidents with much disdain.

And there was small, jolly Georgia Dunbar of Leadville, who usually had too much whiskey, but always had a good time. The *Leadville Evening Chronicle* of January 31, 1883 recorded one such event in Georgia's seemingly carefree life:

> *Last night Georgia Dunbar, an inmate of a house of ill fame on West Fifth street, filled herself full of whiskey . . . and had reached that state of hilarity in which she was insensible to the cold. She proceeded to undress herself for the purpose of a walk . . . denuding her person, she started up West Fifth street . . . she landed in a snow bank three feet deep. This had the effect of cooling the inebriated Georgia off. While she floundered in the snow bank, officer W. Milner came along and assisted her . . . she was taken home and allowed to dress herself, and then escorted to the police station, where she was booked for drunkenness. This morning Judge Rose assessed her a modest fine.*

As is the case today, occasionally, newspaper accounts were in error. For example, Denver denizen Mattie Young, a known alcoholic, often graced the crime sections of the local papers. In August of 1878, while in a drunken state, her buggy overturned, injuring Mattie and her companions. When she died a few days later, the local papers had a field day. Through either bad information or yellow journalism, it was reported that the late Mattie Young was actually Calamity Jane!

In Creede, the leading madam was known as "Creede Lil."[2] Lil began her wayward career in Leadville, in the early 1880s. By 1901, she had made her way to Denver, where she was known on Market Street as Lillis Lovell.

The daughter of a Nebraska farmer, Lillis Lovell was born Emma Lillis Quigley in October 1864. That much has been obtained from court records and her obituary in *The Denver Post*. Nothing else about her past life is known.

Upon her arrival in Denver, she leased Jennie Rogers' house at 2020 Market Street. Lillis was a beautiful woman with a strong head for business. Never the prominent status of Mattie Silks or Jennie Rogers, Lillis did well in her own right. She wore the finest clothes adorned with jewelry rich in diamonds. Expenditures in house decorations ran into thousands of dollars. Through it all, her business flourished. Newspaper accounts of the time suggest the press had a special fondness for this pretty lady of the tenderloin.

Lillis Lovell died of pneumonia on March 22, 1907, at St. Joseph's Hospital. She was forty-two years old. Following cremation at Riverside Cemetery, her estate, originally reported in the newspapers as fifty thousand dollars, was settled for $12,000.

The Ryan family was a dynasty of sorts on Denver's Market Street. Mrs. Jane Elizabeth Ryan ran several saloons and bordellos in Colorado's mining camps before finally settling in Denver. On Market Street, the family ran a bordello, where daughters Julia, Mona, and Annie worked for their madam mother, while son Jim ran a nearby saloon at 20th and Market Street. Jim Ryan's saloon was the scene of a double murder on August 13, 1899. A disgruntled military man named Wellington C. Llewellen shot and killed two policemen, Thomas Clifford and William Griffith. Llewellen fled Ryan's saloon and an intense manhunt gripped Market Street until the killer was caught.

Meanwhile, Jim's sister, a known prostitute, Annie, had a long-term affair with ex-cop Maurice Lyons, who worked as a bartender for Jim. One night in 1909, the two lovers quarreled. Annie took a shot at Maurice but missed. Some twenty years later, Annie shot him again, this time killing him. She was eventually found not guilty.

The story of Molly Foley may be said to be typical of Colorado's Victorian prostitutes. Molly was born in Scotland in 1836. It is said she was fairly tall and quite attractive and popular among the girls she worked with on the line. Molly worked in various mining camps from Chama, New Mexico, to Animas City and Durango, Colorado, long before she came to Silverton in 1878. In Silverton, Molly ran an over-sized crib, by crib standards, and employed two girls. At the age of forty-two, Molly employed girls for service; however, in the nature of the business, Molly herself was considered "less desirable" by the majority of customers.

Molly seemed to have had her fair share of troubles over the years, or so the headlines of the Silverton papers suggest:

Several of the keepers of Blair Street resorts have recently been disregarding the ordinances of the town of Silverton by selling beer without procuring a town license. Molly Foley was arrested Thursday upon a charge of this character and was tried yesterday before Justice B. O'Driscoll. The evidence was not sufficient to warrant conviction; the prisoner was discharged.

A year later, Molly was in trouble again, and the press had a field day, as the *San Juan Democrat* reported on November 10, 1888:

Two fair but frail maidens of Blair Street fame sailing under the euphonious titles of Molly Foley and Lizzie Fisher, had a slight altercation last Saturday, and they proceeded to demolish each other with Spartan-like heroism. Molly led off with a vicious right hander and smote Lizzie in the left optic, almost obscuring her vision. This caused Lizzie's blood to rise ten degrees in the thermometer and she led off with a vicious left-hander on Molly's larder almost knocking the breath of life out of her. Hostilities then ceased for a time, and when they had gotten their breaths, again they proceeded with Sullivan-like viciousness to the combat. Lizzie being shorter and more vicious than her tall antagonist, led off with a wicked left-hander and caromed on Molly's lower ribs, brazing them to the Queen's taste, causing her bustle to stick out too much and bringing tears to her eyes. After recovering from this blow, and now being stung to fury, Molly led out with a paralyzing blow and erected a good sized shanty on the vacant lot between Lizzie's right eye and nose, and painting it a dark blue. At this point the referee declared a draw as Jow Martin and Marshal Snowden were hovering around, and the procession halted. The trouble arose over one of them wounding the young and tender affections of the other.[3]

A *Leadville Chronicle* reporter obviously took great joy in writing the following:

Anyone who passed the famous free-love headquarters on Carbonate avenue, (sic) presided over by Madam W. Purdy, at about five o'clock last evening, heard a big noise. A few of the French-female free-to-be-loved inmates had all become infatuated with one red-headed man. They liked his nicely kept moustache, cleanly shaven chin…and each and every one was not only willing but anxious to fight for him. And they did in a female war. Some with finger nails, others used tall shoe heels, and still others took up hatchets in his defense.
The sequel was seen when Deputy Sheriff Miller was walking towards the Pine street tombs, surrounded by a great lot of red-head infatuated girls. Some of them were put under bonds to come again this evening for trial.

Competition among the girls of the row was often high and venomous. A story often related in Leadville history is that of the girls in the Red Light Dance Hall, in a feud with the girls of the *Bon Ton Dance Hall*. What started as a skirmish over skirt lengths proceeded through a midnight peace talk, with the alcohol flowing freely. A vote was cast with the result of a battle cry unanimous in "war to the knife and knife to the hilt." The female cat fight spilled into the dirt street and soon became bloody, with biting, gouging, punching, hair pulling, spitting and stomping. A few brave patrolmen managed to break up the ruckus and hauled a few to jail. The short skirt scuffle was never resolved. However, the red light district was a bit more peaceful for a time.

The reports of soiled doves fighting among themselves continued, as this example from the *Silverton Standard* demonstrates:

Madam Molly Foley contributed $50 to the city this week for trying to reduce a companion's expenses this winter by fixing her head so that they could eat hay.

From the *Pueblo Chieftain* of August 10, 1872, we learn of the disdain the paper had for their local soiled doves:

A couple of abandoned women at the Hotel de Omaha had a misunderstanding that culminated in a regular street fight. They rolled and tumbled in the mud, pulled hair, fought, bit, gouged and pommeled each other and filled the air with blood-curdling oaths. None of the police officers were on hand to interfere. It was a disgraceful spectacle, and a strong illustration of the morals on the banks of the Arkansas.

Respectability for the ladies of the tenderloin was slow in coming, but a form of respect, if just a matter of getting along, eventually did develop. That respect came from both sides of the line, so to speak, working together. A great example happened at Cripple Creek, shortly after the gold strike of 1891.

Cripple Creek's first Sunday School sermon turned into an embarrassing and somewhat humorous affair. Held in the back of the Buckhorn Saloon, it was up to the proprietor to ready the saloon for the Sunday morning meeting. In this case, the proprietor was Mother Duffy, as the beloved madam was affectionately known. Mother Duffy had the place clean and orderly, with the side benches moved over the dance floor in neat rows. The bar had been covered with a clean sheet of canvas by the time Mother Duffy's girls came downstairs, all dressed in respectable

Allan G. Bird collection

The *Tremont Saloon*, on Silverton's infamous Blair Street, was a popular bordello, run by Big Tillie, who stands to the left. Note the lovely lady borders in the windows above.

Jane Elizabeth Ryan, (seated) ran a bordello with her three daughters as the main attraction. Annie, shown on the right would be charged with murder. Jane Elizabeth's son, Jim, witnessed murder in his saloon.

Girls will be girls, as the soiled doves of Market Street show that there is always time to have fun.

Pearl Thompson, also known as "21 Pearl," a madam of Silverton's Blair Street, was often the victim of childish pranks by nearby youngsters. This photo graces her tombstone in the Silverton cemetery.

Allan G. Bird collection

Denver Public Library

Central City's red light district was moved to this remote industrial section of town following a citizen uproar.

calico dresses. As they took their places along with the rest of the congregation, the sermon began.

No sooner had Father Volpe finished his opening prayer, a commotion from the street entrance held everyone's attention. A drunken old sot wandered in and loudly demanded a drink. Mother Duffy immediately took control of the situation. Mother Duffy was a rather large woman who handled bar fights so well, she had no need for male help. Her vocabulary was said to be quite seasoned as well. Mother Duffy, purple with rage, thundered across the room toward the drunk. "I'll show you, you low-down drunken bum, not to bust up the first Sunday School ever held in this camp! Now get out of here, damn your soul!" With that, Mother Duffy grabbed the drunk by his collar, dragged him to the door and heaved him across the walkway and into the street![4] It is safe to conclude that the Sunday School sermon continued uninterrupted.

Tip Toe Through the Tulips

The girls of Denver's Market Street were still having fun, when in 1882, the celebrated poet and orator Oscar Wilde was scheduled to appear in town. A publicity poster depicted a strange looking man in knee britches gazing at lily flowers. It seems the girls of Market Street had little use for someone they viewed as an effeminate flower lover. Knowing Wilde's particular fondness for sunflowers and lilies, parlor houses and cribs along the tenderloin district decorated elaborately with those blooms. But the prostitutes didn't stop there. Minnie Clifford and Emma Nelson paraded about town, with one wearing "upon her hat, between the port gangway and ridder chains, an immense sunflower fully a foot in diameter, while the other was sporting an immense and very intense lily."[5] The girls chanted such phrases as "too, too divine," and "too utterly utter." Several onlookers applauded with approval as the girls paraded down the street.

It seems the girls weren't the only ones having fun in the good old days before the reform movement brought such a tense atmosphere to many towns in Colorado. Back then, things were more open and at least honest. The *Rocky News* reported:

> . . . a new fashionable den of prostitution on Holladay Street has been opened . . . it was reported that the city council delayed the day session . . . as most of the councilmen were in attendance at the Holladay Street opening.

During Denver's formidable years, Holladay Street was first named McGaa Street, for William McGaa, a local pioneer. The street was later named Holladay Street in honor of Ben Holladay, a pioneer in travel and stagecoach operations. However, by the 1870s, upper Holladay Street had gained a reputation as ". . . one of the Wickedest streets in the West."[6] Thus in 1888, the Holladay family asked the city council to rename the street. They did; to Market Street. So named, according to the council, for the meat markets located on the lower end of the street. Who says politicians don't have a sense of humor? In any case, in an effort to avoid confusion, the famous Denver street will be referred to throughout this work as Market Street.

≥ᴑ Complex, tragic and often circumstantial, could well sum up the lives of many of Colorado's prostitutes. Such is the story of Lizzie Preston. Born in the South in 1839, she was christened Hannah by her parents.[7] Very little is known of her life before Denver. Shortly after the Civil War, she married a veteran by the name of Foster, in Louisiana.

In 1874, the couple began adoption proceedings for a fourteen-month-old infant girl from Saint Anne's Infant Asylum in Washington, D.C. The happy family returned to Louisiana with the intent to complete the adoption. However, health problems due to Mr. Foster's tuberculosis caused the family to move west. Shortly after their arrival in Denver, Mr. Foster died.

Forced to make a living for herself and her infant child, Lizzie Preston, as she was now known, used what little savings she had and purchased a "ladies boarding house" at 23rd and Lawrence. What she bought was a bordello. Circumstance brought Lizzie into the world of prostitution.

A very determined, if not financially desperate woman, Lizzie continued the business of her newly acquired property, thereby becoming Denver's first established madam. She obviously had a head for business, for as the house soon became profitable, Lizzie bought a home at 3051 Stout Street, in which to raise her adopted daughter. Lizzie now led a double life, a life that would eventually haunt her beyond the grave.

Lizzie managed to do well professionally and personally. Her establishment was so successful that within a year, Lizzie purchased property on Market Street, in Denver's leading commercial area and the heart of Denver's red light district.

It was during this time that another future madam of Denver's "row," Mattie Silks, began a friendship and later a business arrangement with Lizzie. Lizzie and her bordello became the most reputable business in the red light district. So much so that by 1876 when Mattie decided to relocate her own business of pleasure, she sought the advice of Lizzie, who by this time knew which politicians, city officials, and police officers could be bribed or otherwise paid off. In the end, Mattie leased one of Lizzie's houses on Market Street. Among the girls in Lizzie's employ was Ella Watson, who went on to operate her own "hog ranch" in Sweetwater, Wyoming, where she was known as "Cattle Kate."

With her business firmly rooted in the heart of Denver's tenderloin area, Lizzie turned her attention to her adopted daughter. By the time young Essie May turned thirteen, it became clear to Lizzie that her secret or "other" life would eventually be known, so she sent the child to a convent in Chicago where she would get a respectable education and Lizzie would have time to sort out her affairs.

Perhaps one of Colorado's most famous tales involving a house of ill-repute occurred at Lizzie Preston's house at 1943 Market Street.8 The tale also involved the beautiful and legendary Baby Doe and her lover at the time, Colorado's Silver King, Horace A. W. Tabor.

March of 1880 was unusually cold in the city. Nevertheless, late one evening, Lizzie received two gentlemen callers into the parlor. They were Harvey Doe, Baby's husband, and a "business associate." Shortly after the two entered the bordello, a second knock was sounded at the door. A woman, possibly Lizzie herself, answered the knock only to be confronted by a very upset Baby Doe and a police officer. The two found Harvey in the company of a young harlot.

Rumors of a set up abounded, particularly by Harvey Doe, who claimed he did not realize Lizzie's house on Market Street was a house of ill repute. True or not, and highly unlikely, this was all Baby Doe needed. With the evidence in hand, including witnesses, the needed evidence was now in hand for the beautiful Baby Doe to secure her divorce from Harvey and clear the way toward marriage with the rich Tabor. Thus, Lizzie played a small part in the most legendary love story in Colorado history.

In 1892, Lizzie's adopted daughter, Essie May returned from five years in a series of convents, only to surprise her mother at her house on Market Street. Realizing the true life her mother led, Essie May denounced Lizzie and never spoke to her again. Some accounts claim she turned to prostitution to get back at her mother, but there is no evidence to back up the story.9

In any case, Essie May's name did surface for the record in 1904. That was the year Lizzie Preston died at age sixty-five. She had only recently acquired a new property at 1942 Market Street, across the street from one of her first houses. It was this new property that would go on to become the most famous of Denver's bordellos, *The House of Mirrors*, thus ensuring Lizzie's place in history.

Lizzie Preston left an estate valued at $25,000 in real estate and jewels, a considerable sum in those days. No less than twenty people came forth laying claim to the fortune of the former madam whom they did not claim when she was living. Among those filing suit to claim the estate was Essie May.

During the lawsuit, records were produced proving that not only was Essie May Foster adopted, a fact she had never been told, but that the adoption was never legally completed. The court denied her claim and the estate of Lizzie Preston (Hannah E. Foster) was sold during probate.10 Among Lizzie's possessions was a pure gold, diamond studded cross valued at $900. Mattie Silks bought this cross which later became her trademark.

Perhaps it was one madam's tribute to another who had gone before.

By the turn of the century, Victorian family life had somewhat settled in picturesque Silverton. Prostitution, still in existence, had taken a turn in town favor, as far as the new social elite was concerned. The following story is a humorous tale of social shenanigans.

The *Mikado* was a small bordello, dance hall and saloon, typical of Silverton's Blair Street. Pearl Thompson, known as "21 Pearl," and Frances Belmont were joint madams of the house, for which they paid cash in 1925.

"21 Pearl" had a little dog that she cherished. This known fact was not lost on a few playful Silverton boys. The boys would snatch the dog and hide it away for a period of time and then walk casually back to the *Mikado* pretending to be "just walking by." Pearl would run out of the bordello in a hysterical state and ask the boys if they had seen her dog, which they denied. Pearl would offer the boys a handsome sum of cash (about $5) if they could find her beloved dog. Presently, the boys would return with the dog and collect their reward. A month or two would pass and the boys would repeat the dog trick and receive another reward. The routine was continued for quite some time. Pearl never did figure out the rouse and the boys had the last laugh . . . as well as the cash.

One of Pearl's girls at the Mikado was Betty Wagner. Known as "Big Billie," she haled from the Telluride tenderloin, where she was known as a kind and generous person. Once again a few of Silverton's mischievous youngsters endeavored to pull a prank on Halloween night. The boys thought it would be great fun to steal the outhouse from the Mikado property. When they set about removing the out-house, they ran into a problem: the small structure was bolted into the ground! Using their teenage brute force, the boys managed to raise a loud ruckus, rather than the outhouse. Investigating the noise, Big Billie came out the back door of the bordello with a shotgun in hand. She ordered the "little S.O.B.s" to get out of there, shooting her weapon well above the fleeing boys. Needless to say, Big Billie gained an amount of guarded respect from the boys.

In Breckenridge, there was confusion at the end of the line. An elderly gentle-man who owned property next to the crib area, erected a framework of sorts around his well. The problem came when drunken customers of the cribs mistook the structure for an outhouse!

❧ Of course, there were always the tenderloin ladies who got into trouble with the law. Old newspaper accounts can often be sad, tragic, humorous, and strange, as this account from a Cripple Creek newspaper shows:

> *Louis Harder and Ethel Brown, . . . are confined to the city jail as a result of a carving Ethel gave Louis in her apartment in Poverty Gulch at 2:00 this morn-ing. Neither will tell how it happened but the marks left on the man's body prove that the woman was adept in the use of a razor. He has 6 marks on his body made by the razor and the skin is peeled off one of his fingers which the woman did with her teeth. He also has tooth marks on his nose.*

From the Central City Register Call, dated May 25, 1883, the following article shows the reporter must have had a sense of humor:

> *A miner had pulled his gun and fired several shots at one of the "fallen angels" who inhabited the Pine Street residence of Ada Branch. Sheriff Williams arrested him and took him off to jail. He appeared before Justice Jones and was fined $60.00 and costs. The entire story is to be dramatized and performed at the opera house at a future date.*

Despite the stately reputation of the *Strater Hotel*, Durango's finest established citizens could not escape the passion of human nature. The fourth floor of the hotel was an unfinished mess with bare floors and little heat. The hotel manage-ment, in their wisdom, deemed this floor the perfect place for their maids' quarters. With make shift walls of draped canvas and blankets, a bit of privacy could be had. What took place after working hours and between the sheets, so to speak, became the talk of the gossip circles. "Monkey Hall" became the name given to the fourth floor of the *Strater Hotel*. It seems that although no men were allowed on the floor, they somehow found their way and "monkey business" took over. The hotel manager did his best to keep up the hotel's fine image, however the hotel's secret floor of sin was no longer a secret.

IN LAW ENFORCEMENT, THERE WAS a fine line between enforcing compliance and outright control, when it came to prostitution. In many towns the budget came almost entirely from license fees, permits, and fines levied against prostitutes and gambling establishments. Thus, regulating the prostitution trade often times crossed a fine line, in more ways than one.

Famed Colorado lawman Cyrus Shores must have dealt with several prostitutes among his many duties. Evidently the good lawman had a kind heart as well. Molly Foley is one example, who always seemed to find trouble. After her days in Silverton, Molly gave Denver a try. Down on her luck, she wrote to her friend Cyrus Shores, asking for money for train fare out of Denver.

On the other hand, Marshal Jim Clark of Telluride, detested prostitutes. On one occasion, as Clark was patrolling the red light district, he encountered one of the prostitutes with her dog. The woman told Clark the dog was old and asked if the marshal would mind taking the dog out sometime and killing him. With that, Clark pulled his gun and shot the dog. The woman's scream could be heard as Clark calmly walked away.

While Clark's disdain for prostitutes is plain, when he was mortally wounded on the streets of Telluride in an ambush, he crawled for help to a nearby crib, where he died.

As frontier law and justice formed and melded, special interests took their issues, picking and choosing more to their liking, than the citizens' interests. Sound familiar?

The laws regarding the prostitution trade were so broad as to be obscure, thereby allowing any particular law officer, council or court to bend either way, very liberally. For example, disturbing the peace and public drunkenness were chargeable offenses. Yet, when officials chose to raid a bordello, these same offenses applied, even though the said prostitute was inside the bordello. And of course, because it was a raid, the fine and court costs were much higher.

Leadville Mayor Humphreys and his city council found themselves in a bit of a financial crunch in the summer of 1880. In an effort to boost the city coffers, an elaborate police raid was set into motion. The *Leadville Evening Chronicle* of October 8, 1880, began their lengthy article this way:

> *There is weeping of glass eyes, gnashing of teeth and tearing of mohair switches in four of the gilded, not to say the brass-mounted palaces of sin of Leadville to-day, (sic). Last night at the silent hour of twelve, when the clocks strike loudest and longest, the police force divided themselves into four squads and proceeded to the well-known mansions of Mollie May, on Fifth street, Sallie Purple, next door, Frankie Paige, on West Fourth street, and Carrie Linnel, on State street . . . the girls were taken somewhat by surprise and the majority of them were not dressed to see company, but the restless coppers ordered them to jail . . . where they were booked and fined $25 and required to show up for trial . . . the true inwardness of the raid is rather peculiar, and the municipal court concerning the houses of ill-fame is original not to say unique.*

The year 1886 was an election year in Colorado. It was also a time when reform movements were gaining support. So it came as no surprise when the Denver police force, on direction from the mayor, raided several bordellos in the tenderloin district. The raids continued throughout the campaign season. What the Denver politicos didn't count on, was the resistance of the madams. Following the election, our ladies of the tenderloin joined in force, elected Jennie Rogers to head the group and informed the Denver courts that if they were convicted of the fines charged during these raids, they would take their cases to the Supreme Court. Of course the newspapers reported on the proceedings with much delight and spicy commentary. In the end, most of the madams charged were fined for lesser charges and the matter was dropped.

Bordello madams were fined fifteen dollars and, each prostitute was assessed a five dollar fee per month, due at the first of each month. By paying this fee, it was generally assumed the individual bordello would not be raided. Police Chief Watson said the prostitutes did not pay their fees until after the twentieth of the month, and as the police department depended on these fees to pay the salary of the officers, they felt "an example needed to be made." The same paper updated the story a few weeks later, stating in part:

The night patrol will hereafter prowl the alleys every half hour, and the other half hour will be spent in mustering up the courage for the operation.

Despite the obstacles, and there were many in a male-dominated camp, the soiled doves were considered a needed commodity. Victorian family life had not yet made its way to all of the mining camps of Colorado. The women of the demimonde provided a service, as well as economic returns for the men who ran the camps. Yet, they often managed to deliver service with a smile despite occasional obstacles.

Parlor houses were big business in Cripple Creek, as in any mining camp. Originally situated near the many saloons along Bennett Avenue (the main street), Marshal Hi Wilson moved the girls and their establishments one block south, on Myers Avenue. In doing so, he managed to keep the peace between the ladies and the business establishment. He promised the city that the ladies would pay a head tax which would be donated to church funds, and, to increase city revenue, the madams would pay a sixteen dollar monthly tax, and each girl would pay a six dollar monthly tax. In this way, the madams and their girls contributed quite handsomely to the town coffers. All girls would receive monthly medical examinations and be required to shop Bennett Avenue's clothing stores in "off hours," thereby not offending the decent citizens of Cripple Creek. Marshal Wilson was simply complying with the trend of the time by relocating the row or the line, off the mining camp's main street.

In Boulder, prostitution and gambling were declared illegal in 1873, yet that did not seem to hinder business in the least. Many houses of ill-repute were on land owned by prominent businessmen. Knowing a good profit when they pocketed it, these men of Boulder knew how to circumvent the laws. By 1878, these very men had the law repealed and prostitution flourished.

In Gilpin County, where gold had been discovered, starting the whole crazy mad-dash to Colorado Territory in 1858, Central City became an overnight mining camp. Hundreds of miners poured into the area. By 1860, a new frame building had been erected on a new street in the new town. Gold had brought prosperity and decency to Central City. The citizens of Central City were quite proud of their early development until the local paper reported the business activities of the new building:

. . . a sort of hurdy gurdy saloon, built of rough logs and containing the usual primitive accessories of a dance house, viz: (sic) a bar well stocked with Taos Light-ning, (sic) a few benches and tables, and three or four girls educated in the business of passing drinks and bandying course epithets with whomsoever pleased to call them out. There was music, whiskey, cards, &c., (sic) and an occasional shooting match inside to vary the monotony of things. Women of any kind were scarce in those days, and the saloon was therefore well patronized.

In 1868, the red light district of Central City was moved to the southern edge of town.

From time to time, community support of the soiled doves did surface. In 1871, a women's church group in Denver offered a redemption program of sorts. The program provided room and board with church members in return for domestic duties. The program never got past the church pulpit. The *Rocky Mountain News* blasted the idea by suggesting the prostitutes of Denver would be better off in asylums and further suggested that if they went to *"good Christian homes,"* the purity of women would be shattered.

As social virtues emerged in the forming towns of early Colorado, health issues among the prostitutes became a platform among the reformers. Our ladies of the tenderloin had been dealing with this for years. Venereal disease was always a major concern, for health as well as business. A prostitute "burned" was detrimental to her business. The soiled doves were very much aware of disease and took what measures they could, when they could. Douches were used as often as practical and if not practical, often times extra doses of "medication" were added to a douche mixture. Additives included bichloride of mercury, mercury cyanide, carbolic acid, and later, lysol, bleach and hydrogen peroxide.

By the 1880s Colorado's medical board, in conjunction with local law enforcement agencies, instituted monthly examinations of all prostitutes at an average charge of two dollars. Doctor Harry Thomas of Victor also treated any known customers of the occasional prostitute diagnosed with venereal disease.

Undoubtedly, many doctors were concerned about their personal practice and reputation once they were known to be treating the local prostitutes. One doctor in particular eventually lost his practice. Doctor J. N. Hall treated the popular Denver madam Jennie Rogers until her death in 1909 of uremic poisoning.[11] The good doctor later died alone, in a poor house.

THE OLD RUGGED CROSS

Mining communities typically buried their "lower class" unceremoniously. Many communities laid out separate sections in their cemeteries called the "potter's field." These sections were reserved for prostitutes, black people, gunslingers and gamblers, or any other person the town wished to classify as undesirable. Thus, many of our ladies are buried in remote sections of cemeteries, and most without headstones.But exceptions were made.

Telluride held an impressive funeral of its own on August 25, 1899. The *Telluride Journal* reported:

> . . . the procession followed the remains of Mabel Walker to the cemetery yesterday. The pallbearers were women. Six of her sisters in shame, tastily attired in modest gowns of black, each wearing a bow of white crepe on the left arm, walking on either side of the hearse to the Methodist church and thence to the cemetery. It was a modestly conducted funeral and gave evidence that, though ostracized from society, these unfortunates have a very tender feeling for their fellow unfortunates.

Almost without exception, our ladies of the tenderloin who died sad and even tragic deaths did not have enough money to pay for even the simplest of funerals.

> A woman, one of Blair Street's unfortunates, known as May Rikard, died in the cabin of Molly Foley without friends or home, after a night of carousing at one of the dance halls, laid down on her bed and sank into her last sleep. Very likely the world has been but a channel house of blasted hopes to her years and, without doubt, the transition from a living death to the grave, were a relief. All of these fallen women have heart histories, dating backward from the childhood's happy hour to the bleak existence cast upon them later on. Repentance is an easy word and conveys a lot of meaning. In the case of the fallen women, however, there's generally an insurmountable barrier to its attainment. Not often does the cloak of charity fall from a sneering, pelting world upon a Magdalene. The body was examined by Coroner Prosser and County Physician Prewitt, no marks of violence were found upon it. Mr. Prosser's opinion was that the woman died from alcoholism. The deceased, it is stated by those living with her, said she had taken a dose of morphine about midnight. No inquest was held and the remains were buried by acquaintances who solicited subscriptions for that purpose.

Sadie Doyle was considered old by prostitution standards when she arrived at Denver's Union Station in 1893. Although thirty years old, she was still pretty and very determined. Sadie headed for Market Street where she gained employment in one of the bordellos of that infamous red light district. Sadie did well in Denver and unlike many of her soiled sisters, she saved her money. She was known as a kind, friendly person and had many friends, including Miss Laura Evans and Lillian Powers.

In later years, Sadie roomed with Annie Ryan, a fellow soiled dove, and member of the famed Ryan family of Market Street. One night while Annie was in the adjoining room with a customer, a fight broke out. Sadie, who now was blind, tried to reach the room to help Annie, when a shot rang out. Annie had shot Maurice Lyons, a Denver policeman who was Annie's lover for several years. Both Annie and Sadie were taken to jail, but were later released when the court ruled the shooting was self defense.

Following the reform and subsequent prohibition laws of 1916 and 1919, Sadie was glad she had saved her earnings. She started a call-girl service on Arapahoe Street, which she ran from her small apartment, filled with singing song birds, for Sadie loved their cheerful company. What she did not like however, was this new way of business. Sadie was of the old school of prostitution, which was that the customer always came to the prostitute. With this new call-girl operation, the girls now went to the customer, which Sadie did not think was safe. However, the new reform laws had changed all that.

In August of 1949, Sadie was arrested for operating a "den of prostitution," and according to the new laws, forced to dissolve her business. If Sadie didn't give up her operation following the arrest, she appeared to have done so; at least the law thought so. In a 1948 interview, Lillian Powers recalled her friendship with Sadie:

Yes I knew (Blind Sadie,) poor soul. She was a very nice looking woman the first time I saw her, and before she went blind, and she had the most beautiful hands I ever saw — my, what pretty hands. I was up to see her about a year and a half before she died. Poor soul. And you know, I hated to go there because she'd cry when I'd leave. Ya know I'd known her so long. I used to know her when she was still down on the line.

On October 1, 1950, Sadie Doyle died in Denver. Her funeral service was brief, the attendance was small, but when a singer sang the words to *The Old Rugged Cross*, the tears were many and the sorrow was heartfelt.

End Notes: Chapter Two

1 San Juan County Historical Society
2 This is not be confused with Creede Lilly.
3 *San Juan Democrat*, September 3, 1887, and November 10, 1888.
4 Sprague, *Money Mountain*
5 *The Rocky Mountain News*, April 5, 1882.
6 Parkhill, *The Wildest of the West*.
7 Denver County Court Probate records.
8 The house was 433 Holladay Street before the change to 1943 Market Street, directly across the street from the famous House of Mirrors.
9 There is the possibility she used a different name, in which case identity is questionable at best.
10 Arapahoe County Archives, and the *Denver Times*, October 09, 1905.
11 A kidney disease due to abnormalities in the blood.

THREE

*"There is something very attractive to men about a madam.
She combines the brains of a businessman, the toughness of a prize fighter,
the warmth of a companion, the humor of a tragedian.
Myths collect about her."* — John Steinbeck

*"I was never legally married, never pregnant, never burned, and I have no
regrets."*
— Lillian Powers

Queens of the Row

The capital city of Denver, along with most of Colorado, was booming in the 1880s. A bit removed from the downtown financial district, Denver's Market Street was doing a great business as well. With the many houses of ill-repute along Denver's tenderloin district, the *House of Mirrors* reigned supreme among all others and would directly involve the best known madams in all of Colorado.

Denver's glamorous madam Jennie Rogers, about the time she built her infamous *House of Mirrors* on Market Street.

Although no interior photographs from that time exist, by all accounts the *House of Mirrors* was the finest parlor house west of the Mississippi. Rumors of blackmail, deceit, and murder surrounded a $17,000 loan Market Street madam Jennie Rogers obtained for her new house business.

Jennie Rogers purchased the house at 1942 Market Street in 1889, and hired renowned architect William Quale to remodel the entire building. Some of Quale's other work included a Denver high school, a church, and several mansions. He carried his workmanship forward in this masterpiece. The exterior gray stone masonry was capped with five facial sculptures, carved in Colorado red stone.

Inside, entire walls and ceilings were covered with mirrors, framed by golden bird's-eye maple. In an interview with historian Fred Mazzulla, Laura Evans, another famous madam on the row, described the famous interior:

> *There was a bird's-eye maple grand piano in the mirrored parlor. The piano was in the southwest corner of the room, and to the left of the fireplace as you entered. There was a tete-'a tete chair, being a chair shaped like the letter S, in the middle of the room under the chandelier. This S shaped chair was covered with white velvet with big embossed red roses with green leaves. It matched the satin carpet on the floor. The woodwork on this chair, and some of the other furniture was of imitation gold. There were two big arm chairs in the room at the front; one in each corner. There was a settee in the other corner in the southeast corner of the room. The beautiful crystal chandelier hung from the middle of the room. Directly south of this parlor was the ballroom. There were mirrors about three feet wide that went from the ceiling to the floor. These mirrors were in oval frames. The frames were carved with figures of nude women. There were electric lights all around the ballroom. The five piece colored orchestra sat on an elevated platform. There were high-backed carved gothic styled chairs around the room. The chairs had big stuffed arms. There were ottomans on each side of the chairs. The girls were permitted to sit only on the ottomans. They were not permitted to sit on the chairs, or on the laps of the gentleman guests.*[1]

The *House of Mirrors* was the envy of all the other madams on the row. Yet, however good the business may have been, the infamous house of ill-repute seemed to hold its own measure of mystery, as well as tragedy for some, and a sense of despair for others. On Market Street, women such as Ella Wellington, Laura Evans, and the legendary Mattie Silks and Jennie Rogers ruled Denver's famous Red Light District. And they all had a connection to the infamous house.

Possibly believing she had finally reached her goal, Jennie Rogers soon lost interest in the *House of Mirrors*. Ella Wellington leased the house from Jennie just two years after it opened. Ella committed suicide in the upstairs chamber less than three years later. Mattie Silks, dethroned as the *Queen of the Row* when Jennie Rogers built the great house, finally reclaimed the title, following the death of Rogers, Mattie bought the famous house from Jennie's estate.

And there was teenager Lillian Powers, already a seasoned prostitute, who met Mattie Silks. The two would have many educational visits in the house. Laura

Evans, who by this time had become a well-known madam, watched the horror gripping Denver as the assailant known as "Jack the Ripper" roamed the tenderloin, killing many girls along the row. She watched as Mattie Silks put bars on all the windows of the *House of Mirrors* to protect the girls, then left Denver and the madness along the tenderloin.

> *It was said that the newly rich speculators, who couldn't stand prosperity, spent their money on the Holladay Street damsels, who couldn't stand posterity.* — Forbes Parkhill[2]

The successful madam had a strong business sense, and was quite charismatic given her Victorian times. Her manner and personal traits, despite her profession, fit in well with her role and her surroundings. In the world of prostitution, the successful madam molded her reputation and adapted to the ways of the underworld. In this way she earned the respect of her professional peers and those around her. She also possessed an intuition in hiring the working girls who had character that would reflect on her business, as well as herself. The woman who succeeded as a madam was truly a remarkable person. The following women were indeed successful madams.

Mattie Silks is considered Denver's first *Queen of the Row*. She was a colorful lady and lived life to the fullest. In appearance, she was short and a bit chunky, yet she dressed in the finest attire and stood tall among her peers in the tenderloin district. Her charm, business acumen, and lust for life are legendary. There are few photographs of the famous madam. In those known to exist, she always is attired in the finest dress with her trademark gold and diamond cross necklace, formerly owned by Lizzie Preston.

Mattie was born Martha Ann Normanm, on April 26, 1845, in Miami County, Indiana. Throughout her life, Mattie rarely spoke of her childhood.[3]

Mattie said in later interviews that she opened her first bordello at the age of nineteen. She claimed she was always a madam and never one of the girls. By the mid 1870s, Mattie decided to head west. To pay for the trip, she worked as a freighter on the wagon trains headed to Colorado from St. Joseph, Missouri. Eventually. she put together a group of soiled doves from cow camps like Abilene and Dodge City. They made their way to the Colorado gold mines, stopping occasionally to set up their canvas tent for business.

By 1875, Mattie and her girls were running a bordello in Georgetown. It was here that Mattie met a gentleman by the name of Silks. Because Mattie took the name Silks and used it for much of her lifetime. It is believed a common law marriage took place: as there is no marriage certificate recorded in the Clear Creek County records. Whatever the marriage arrangement may have been, Mattie left Georgetown in 1877 and Silks left the picture forever. Mattie kept the name Silks and ever after adorned herself in the finest silk fashions.

By 1877, she had moved on to Denver, where she soon made newspaper headlines:

Madame Silks was fined $12 for drunkenness, and paid it like a little woman. She ought to play it finer when she gets on a spree. — Rocky Mountain News, March 28, 1877

The flamboyant Mattie again made the newspapers in August 1877. At a somewhat questionable park just west of the Denver city limits and along the South Platte River (near today's 16th Street viaduct,) a foot race took place with a sizable audience of Denver's soiled dove population on hand as spectators. Mattie placed a large bet on her new love interest, volunteer fireman, turned sprinter, Cortez Thomson. Thomson won the race and the celebration began. Before long, Mattie got into a bit of a scuffle with a another madam, Kate Fulton. According to newspaper accounts, Cortez Thomson intervened by hitting Fulton, possibly breaking her nose, whereupon Fulton's man, Sam Thatcher, stepped in and also was hit by Thomson. With the evening ruined, Mattie and Cortez headed for town in their carriage. During the return trip, a second carriage pulled alongside. Someone fired a gun, barely missing Thomson.

In Denver gossip circles, the story became embellished with every telling. It was said Kate had been too friendly with Cortez Thomson, considered Mattie's man. Mattie, according to the gossips, assuming the shot was a threat, called Kate out to a duel. Both fired their pistols; both missed their targets. To top off the great story, Mattie's bullet nicked a bystander; her beloved Thomson.

Despite the gossip, or because of it, Mattie's business flourished. Mattie ran her fine establishment keenly for twenty years, while other houses came and went. The services and atmosphere were first rate, yet discreet. Denver's finest "carriage" clientele were her customers, including government officials and leading businessmen. Mattie Silks was Denver's first *Queen of the Row*.

As business continued to grow, Mattie's on-again, off-again romance with Cortez Thomson took a turn. Thomson, who had a wife back east, eventually learned she had died. Free to marry Mattie and thus gain legal access to her wealth, Thomson proposed marriage. Mattie, so smart in business, had long ago lost her heart to the drinking, gambling womanizer. The two were married in July 1884. Thomson, with Mattie's money, purchased a ranch near Wray, Colorado and Mattie purchased horses for the ranch. She would take vacations at the ranch and Thomson would visit Denver, usually getting money from Mattie and losing it on gambling and drinking.

Meanwhile, Mattie continued to reign as Market Street's most notable madam. So much so that in 1892, while Denver prepared for its first major convention, the Knights of Templar fraternal organization, a city directory of sorts was published. Mattie, evidently thinking her business was doing well enough, declined to advertise.

Entitled *Denver's Red Book*, the directory was a parody of sorts of the eastern social registers. A register of parlor houses, bordellos and other services, the book advertised fine cigars, elegant furnishings, ample liquors and discretely advertised pretty ladies to the "gentleman in search of relaxation."

Mattie Silks indeed had all the business she could handle. She still owned the original houses she had purchased back in 1877. She had leased them to other madams, yet remained at 1916-1922 Market Street constantly for forty years. She continued to invest in real estate and sold a house at 2009 Market Street to her friend and competitor, Jennie Rogers.

By the 1890s, Mattie was independently wealthy and her husband, Cortez Thomson, was still independently wild. An incident of no small matter occurred when Mattie learned of an affair her husband was having. In a rage, Mattie located the two participants in a local rooming house. Entering the room, an angry Mattie fired her pistol. Her first shot missed the mark and her second shot split the floor boards. The other woman fled the room as Thomson proceeded to beat Mattie. The following day, Mattie filed for divorce in Arapahoe County. Thomson eventually came around and Mattie eventually forgave him.

The couple took a long trip to Alaska, perhaps to mend their marriage; however, Mattie took a few of her girls and did a bit of business during their stay in the far north. Upon their return to Denver, Mattie resumed her business with a new interest in investing her Alaskan earnings. Thomson returned to the ranch in Wray, and his old ways.

In April 1900, Mattie was notified Thomson was quite ill. Rushing to the ranch, Mattie nursed her husband, but to no avail. Cortez Thomson died the next day. Mattie had his body taken to Denver, where he was buried in the stately Fairmount Cemetery.

Mattie returned to her business. A social movement to shut down the parlor houses of Denver gained momentum in 1910. Police raids became common and general harassment escalated.

None of this apparently mattered to Mattie for she boldly paid $14,000 cash for the famed *House of Mirrors*, from the Jennie Rogers estate. Her friend and rival, Rogers, had dethroned Mattie for a time, when she built the house. Now Mattie could reclaim the title of *Queen of the Row*. She did so in an all assuming way. Her customers walked over a beautifully tiled front entrance with the engraved "M. *Silks*" laid in the tile.

Mattie had made her mark.

For a short three years, Mattie reveled as the *Queen of the Row* in the magnificent *House of Mirrors*. In 1916, prohibition took hold of the state and Denver in particular. Mattie turned one of her houses into a hotel and tried to hang on. She finally sold the *House of Mirrors* in 1919. It would become a Buddhist temple and later converted into a warehouse. The glory of this extraordinary house of ill-repute was lost forever.

During prohibition, Mattie, at the age of seventy-six, found love once again. Jack Ready was a large, handsome bordello bouncer. The two began a courtship and Mattie moved "Handsome Jack," as he was known, into her house and made him a manager. The two soon married.

Mattie died from complications suffered during a fall, in 1929. Only a handful of mourners attended her service, followed by burial next to Cortez Thomson, her only true love.

❧ Jennie Rogers was a young friend of Mattie's. She also was a business rival. Jennie was taller and slimmer and perhaps more glamorous than Mattie. Like Mattie, Jennie had her own piece of trademark jewelry. She was almost never seen in public without her shimmering emerald earrings. Yet, Mattie had name recognition and a solid reputation. Jennie learned from Mattie and eventually dethroned her mentor. Jennie Rogers became *Queen of the Row* until her death in 1909.

While Mattie had the recognition, Jennie soon became the most spectacular madam in all of Denver. Leaving St. Louis in a rush and under a cloud of suspicious behavior, Jennie arrived in Denver in 1879, where she was first known as Leah Fries. A doctor's wife, Jennie had run off with a Captain Rogers, who mastered a Missouri River steamboat. In Denver, and minus the captain, Jennie made the acquaintance of Mattie Silks, who became her friend and business rival. Just a few short weeks later, in January of 1880, she paid $4,600 *cash* for her first Market Street house, 2009 Market Street, purchasing it from Mattie Silks. Although the recorded documents bear her legal name, she became known from this moment on as Jennie Rogers. And like Mattie previously, it wasn't long before Jennie made headlines. She was arrested, as *The Rocky Mountain News* reported in March 1880, for "unladylike conduct," and stated she was "well-known in the city."

Jennie loved horses and riding. She would ride in solitude for hours, and other times she could be seen riding a bit recklessly through the streets of Denver. It was all in fun . . . and a bit of advertising as well. It seems to have worked in an area Jennie had not counted on. John A. "Jack" Woods was a hack driver and worked part-time at the horse stables where Jennie frequently rented horses. Eventually, the two fell in love and carried on a torrid affair for years.

With her rising status along Denver's tenderloin district, Jennie expanded her parlor house holdings in 1884 when she built her first house at 1950 Market Street. No madam of the row had ever had a house built on the row. The house was a full three stories. The first floor was decorated in a lavish Middle Eastern flare. Called the Turkish floor, it included a massive receiving room, or parlor, a large ballroom, a dining room, and the kitchen. The second and third floors included an unprecedented fifteen rooms where the women "boarders" lived and, well, worked. One of Denver's fist central furnaces was installed in the basement.

Jennie was now the most popular madam in Denver's tenderloin. With her new house, her business was at an all time high. At the height of her career success, Jennie employed more than twenty girls — more than any other madam in Denver.

Not content with her success, Jennie built the grandest parlor house ever. The *House of Mirrors* became Jennie's crowning jewel on Market Street and all of Denver. Built in 1889, it was mirrored in scandal, yet so resplendent, it became the envy of all the other madams on the row.

Jennie had an old love interest in St. Louis who also happened to be a policeman. On one of his many trips to Denver, Jennie told him of her ambition to own

Denver's finest brothel. The officer conceived of a plan to make Jennie's dream come true. He uncovered secrets in the personal life of a wealthy Denver businessman who had thoughts of running for public office. The enterprising businessman had married, started a family, and served with the Union Army in the Civil War before he came west to Denver and eventual scandal. He acquired an interest in one of the early Denver newspapers as well as an interest in the owner's wife. A short time later, the young entrepreneur's wife was no longer seen at social functions. Tongues wagged, but the young man never offered an explanation for his wife's disappearance. Eventually, the wife of the newspaper owner divorced her husband and married the younger man. The new couple bought out the divorced owner of the newspaper, who never recovered from his personal tragedy.

By the 1880s, the new couple was considered one of the wealthiest families in Denver. Business dealings included the railroad industry, mining, real estate and banking. They also were known for their interest in civic and humanitarian causes. They helped to establish the Denver Public Library, and were instrumental in the founding of the Denver Chamber of Commerce and the Colorado Historical Society.[4]

Colorado was gearing up for an election and the wealthy businessman became interested in running for office. The rumor mongers spread the gossip of the man's past once again, and as gossip goes, added the rumor of murder of the first wife — which brings us back to Jennie and her officer friend from St. Louis. With the rumors running wild and an election looming, the time was right to proceed with the scheme. The officer dug up a skull from an abandoned burial plot and reburied it in the wealthy man's backyard. Later, in police uniform, he appeared at the front door of the man's house. With a forged search warrant in hand, the St. Louis officer stated he was investigating a possible murder. After a short interrogation, the officer went to the backyard and "discovered" the "evidence." Shocked, the wealthy civic leader only mumbled. Letting the man stew a few moments, the officer proceeded with his scheme. The whole thing can be dropped, he said, if the gentleman would pay Jennie Rogers $17,000. The terrified man agreed and paid the officer at once.

Incredibly, there is no evidence that the man's first wife died, nor is there any record of a criminal investigation. Also incredible is that as Jennie's house renovations went over budget, the businessman reportedly paid her the additional amount needed.

Thus the businessman remained a civic leader, but never ran for political office, and Jennie became a civic leader of sorts. And so Jennie's magnificent *House of Mirrors* came into being.

The opening of Jennie's new parlor house at 1942 Market Street was an opulent affair. It offered the finest food and drink, as well as the many tantalizing ladies of the evening. Many Denver dignitaries were said to be present at the party that lasted until dawn. Jennie's business was better than ever. So much so, that a formal entry way was made to connect the parlor house next door, at 1946 Market Street, a house Jennie had obtained by buying out the lease of the tenant, Eva Lewis. Jennie had indeed earned the crown of *Queen of the Row*.

Market Street, and Jennie's house in particular, was only a short walk from the Colorado Legislature at that time. Entire business conventions booked their entertainment at Jennie's houses. David Mechling, a drugstore owner on Larimer Street from 1887 to 1935, told the *Rocky Mountain News*:

> *Each afternoon about three o'clock the august lawmakers would retire to Jennie Roger's Palace of Joy on Market Street and there disport themselves in riotous fashion . . . nothing was thought of that sort of thing in those days.*

Jennie's business thrived and she began investing in real estate north of Denver, including a residential area in the new Sloan's Lake subdivision. She also invested in the new irrigation project in north Logan County which would eventually result in the building of North Sterling Reservoir, a landmark water project on the eastern plains.

By 1884, Jennie's lover, Jack, owned and operated a saloon in Salt Lake City, financed by Jennie's money. The new business did very well, as did the two partners. The two would make frequent "business" trips to either Denver or Salt Lake City, to see each other. One unannounced visit by Jennie, however, turned violent. Upon her arrival, Jennie found her beloved Jack in the arms of another woman. Eternal devotion turned to rage and Jennie pulled out a small pistol and shot and wounded her lover. Arrested and under interrogation, Jennie was asked why she shot Jack. In legendary form, for there are no local newspaper accounts of the incident, Jennie is said to have replied, "I shot him because I love him, damn him!"

Scandal, mystery, sex and intrigue, became the legacy of the famous *House of Mirrors.*

(Opposite) If Jennie was Denver's glamorous madam, Mattie Silks was the reigning *Queen of the Row.* -

Author's collection

Two of the five facial sculptures that graced the *House of Mirrors*. Adding to the legend, they were believed to be the five major players in the blackmail scandal surrounding the famous bordello.

Henrietta Denoyer collection

Bible belonging to Laura Evans dated at the time of her Continuation, during her youth.

A typical Denver bordello and the soiled doves, with a young Laura Evans, seated second from left, about the time she left Denver, frightened by the media dubbed "Murders on the row."

Miss Laura Evans points to the sign posted on her Salida bordello when her prostitution business finally was closed down, in the 1950s. Miss Laura took in male borders and played cards with them, until her death a few years later.

Colorado Historical Society

Lillian Powers, (standing left,) poses with fellow Denver soiled doves. Next to her is Lillis Lovell. The other two women are unidentified.

Historians disagree as to the date of this incident — or if it actually occurred. In any case, it is known Jennie Rogers wed John A. "Jack" Woods in August 1889. The marriage was not a happy one and the two soon went their separate ways.

Meanwhile, Jennie's business was doing so well she afforded a little time for herself. She eventually leased her 1950 Market Street property to Minnie Hall, and spent some time traveling. In 1891, Jennie leased the famous *House of Mirrors* to Ella Wellington. It was also during this time that Jennie's health deteriorated somewhat. Friends suggested rest and relaxation. Jennie was suffering from what was called "melancholy episodes" — depression.

In the ten short years since she had arrived in Denver, she had achieved her every dream, except one. Unending love and happiness. She still had love for Jack Woods and the sad heartache at times became unbearable.

Tragedy struck the *House of Mirrors* in 1894. Jennie had leased the house to Ella Wellington three years previously. Ella did a fine business, but the sad, unhappy lady put a gun to her head. Following her tragic death, Jennie was forced to once again operate the establishment.

In February of 1896, Jennie's beloved Jack died in Omaha, Nebraska. When she learned of his death, Jennie had Jack's body removed to Denver for burial. Jennie paid for the burial plot and tombstone in Denver's Fairmount Cemetery. The gesture was heartfelt, the turnout was dismal.

Jennie returned to her business enterprises, but her heart, and moreover her mind, was no longer up to the task. Falling into another state of melancholy despair, she leased the *House of Mirrors* to Lizzie Preston in late 1896. Within a few short years, Jennie leased out all of her Market Street holdings, the last being the house at 2020 Market Street, a recent purchase, to Verona Baldwin. Using her rental income, she invested in more real estate. In time, Jennie would become rich in real estate investments, and cash poor.

Jennie continued to travel extensively, and in 1902, while in Chicago, she visited a nationally known doctor. Jennie had suffered the past few years from severe headaches and nausea. She was diagnosed with Bright's disease, a serious kidney ailment. Because of the diagnosis, or the doctors, Jennie stayed in Chicago. She borrowed a large sum of money and purchased a lavish parlor house in Chicago's tenderloin district. Collateral used for this investment was a Denver property and Jennie's treasured emerald earrings. The Chicago enterprise was somewhat of a success, as Jennie managed to pay down her debt considerably. It was in her new parlor house that Jennie met a powerful Chicago businessman, Archibald T.

Fitzgerald, twenty years her junior. Fitzgerald lavished Jennie with gifts including jewels, expensive carriages and horses. Two years later, they wed in Hot Springs, Arkansas.

Shortly after the marriage, Jennie learned Denver madam and friend, Lizzie Preston had died. Returning to Denver, Jennie took charge of the *House of Mirrors*. Jennie stayed in Denver two years, during which time she somehow learned of her new husband's true nature. In 1907, she hired a detective to learn more of Fitzgerald's dealings. Fitzgerald had swindled several businessmen out of their holdings and apparently was attempting to secure his wife's Denver properties. Jennie hired an attorney but never filed for divorce. It is possible she simply never got around to it, as her health began to decline rapidly. Business seemed to slack off, and Jennie apparently lost interest. She leased the *House of Mirrors* once again and moved into her 1950 Market Street house where she would remain until her death.

In 1909, Jennie, now sixty-five years old with mounting debts, borrowed what money she could from fellow madams. Her health continued to decline, and eventually she relented to her doctor's advice. Once a vivacious, handsome and smart businesswoman, a frail, broken down Jennie Rogers almost seemed resigned to her fate. However, total bed rest was not in Jennie's nature. She may have given up the fight, for on October 16, 1909, Jennie spent most of the day getting her affairs in order, and finally wrote out her will. She was dead by morning.

Jennie Rogers was buried in Fairmount Cemetery, next to her beloved Jack. Her funeral was one of the largest attended for a member of the soiled dove society. Jennie's legacy remains today.

Even Mattie Silks could not, or would not, take that away from her.

AT THE TIME OF HER death, in April of 1953, Laura Evans had become a true legend in her own time.[5] She was very secretive about her upbringing. We do know she was from the South. Laura married at age seventeen, left her husband (and possibly a child) and headed west for a new life. She originally settled in St. Louis, where she engaged in prostitution. She was in her early twenties when she came to Denver, finding work on Market Street. By the 1890s, she had left Denver for Leadville's silver boom.

Leadville is the town of legends and Laura Evans soon became one. Miss Laura loved to have a good time. She lived life to the fullest and had a devil-may-care attitude. A few of her rollicking good times included a little horseplay, literally. Laura watched the horse-drawn chariots roll into Leadville when the Ringling

Brothers brought their circus act to town. She and another parlor house girl conspired to rent a chariot and a couple of horses by tipping the water boy. Next thing Leadville knew, a horse drawn chariot was speeding out of control, turning onto State Street, charging past the parlor houses and cribs, and then turning down Harrison Avenue, Leadville's main street. Laura tried to round a corner off Harrison Avenue too fast, hit a pole in front of the *Vendome Hotel* and the chariot crashed. Witnesses gasped as Laura tumbled out of the chariot. The police were in the process of arresting her and her cohort when a well-known businessman (and customer of Laura's) intervened. Laura was allowed to leave the scene with no charges filed against her.

Then there was the time in the winter months of 1896, when Laura and her parlor house friend wrecked havoc at Leadville's *Ice Palace*. The *Ice Palace* was built as a tourist attraction at a cost of more than $200,000 — a lot of money in those days — only to melt away come springtime. Laura had the notion to pull her horse-drawn sleigh right into the palace. As the horse and sleigh entered the structure, Laura tried to bring the animal to a halt. The loud music inside the palace, echoing off the ninety-foot ice pillars, startled the horse, who began prancing and kicking.

"He kicked the hell out of our sleigh and broke ice shafts as he ran away. He kicked a four foot ice pillar all to pieces and ruined all the ore exhibits before he ran home to his stable," Laura recalled years later.[6]

Later that same year, Laura became a heroine and true legend in Leadville. A strike occurred at one of Leadville's many mines. Armed troops guarded the area and blocked the road to stop union members. The owners, in an effort to get the payroll to the workers who chose not to strike, asked Miss Laura to smuggle the payroll through the union lines. Laura secured the payroll pouch beneath the layers of her skirts, mounted her horse sidesaddle, and rode up Carbonate Hill. As most men knew Laura from her State Street parlor house, she simply smiled sweetly and explained she wanted to visit a friend who hadn't been allowed to leave the mine on account of the strike. The guards let her pass and she safely relayed the payroll to the superintendent. Laura later recalled that the owner was so grateful as the payroll broke the strike that she was asked to dinner at the owner's home. When she arrived at the dinner party, she was introduced as a business associate, and discreetly given a $100 dollar bill as she left.

Although high spirited to a fault, for all her pranks and follies, Laura possessed a strong and serious nature. Despite her chosen profession, or because of it, Laura had a confidence and a strong will unmatched by any other woman in the business. She has been described as kind and generous, strict and calculated. She was bold, wild, boisterous with her profanity, and quick with a keen wit. She rolled her own cigarettes and kept her money in her stocking. She had a great sense of humor, a colorful manner and at times her language would equal any miners' use of the four-letter words. It is said she was quite a beauty in her younger days. Her dark eyes remained clear and twinkling throughout her life.

By 1898 Laura was back on Market Street. She had graduated from a parlor house girl in Leadville, to a madam on Denver's famous red light district, with the likes of Jennie Rogers and Mattie Silks. However, Laura's boisterous personality and flamboyant characteristics soon became legend. Her brass check from Leadville reads: "Eat, drink, dance, go to bed, or get out."[7]

Laura's business did very well. She was strict with her girls, yet she gained their respect. Laura believed in health and cleanliness and her girls were required to keep themselves and their rooms clean and neat. Laura's girls were young, attractive, and experienced. From a taped interview of *LaVerne* by Fred Mazzulla, one of the women who worked for her said:

Miss Laura was always so strict about such things and keeping her reputation and she'd have us girls be regularly inspected by a doctor. As I said before, everyone loved Miss Laura.[8]

Although she did a good business in Denver, Laura was in constant competition with Mattie Silks and Jennie Rogers. Laura once called Mattie Silks' house "The Old Ladies Roost."[9] Mattie was loyal to her older girls and kept them in her employ well past their prime. While Miss Laura's statement was a bit vindictive, it was said against a business rival. In actuality, Miss Laura cared for her girls, too. When the girls were no longer bringing in clientele, Miss Laura secured employment for them in reputable establishments or in other bordellos.

Shortly after the turn of the century, Laura Evans left Denver for good. Terror gripped Market Street. A series of unsolved murders in and around the red light district left everyone in a near state of panic. Denver newspapers dubbed the unknown murderer, "Jack the Ripper," which only heightened the fear.[10]

In an interview with Fred Mazulla just months before her death in 1953, Laura said:

The reason I left Denver when I did was because Jack the Ripper was cutting the wombs out of some of the girls. Even before Jack the Ripper, boarding houses had bars on the windows. But poor Mattie Silks, when she put bars on the upper windows, her girls got scared and her business never recovered.

Laura moved to the small mountain town of Salida. Salida was a railroad town, full of men, and men meant business. Laura did so well in her Front Street house that by 1906 she bought the row of cribs across the street. Laura slowly endeared herself to the elite businessmen of Salida. By now, Laura's reputation as a kind and caring madam had spread statewide. Lillian Powers recalled years later:

I had never seen Miss Laura but I heard about her, and I knew there was a vacancy, so I called her up. She said she had just one place left. I told her I couldn't come for a few days and she said it would be alright, she would save it for me. When I got there, I offered to pay the back rent, but she wouldn't let me.[11]

This phone call was taken at Laura's house, where she had installed a pay phone, the first in the state.

In another act of kindness in Salida, Miss Laura also showed her characteristic matter of fact thoughts. Laura related in a 1950 interview that she was once approached by the religious crusaders. Laura gave them each a five dollar bill, and said, "Don't bother with me. I've got a one-way ticket to hell. Take care of these younger folks, they can use you." True to form, Laura said it as she saw it.

Laura's business floundered during Prohibition and was eventually shut down. Laura's house of ill repute was the last in the state to close. Laura eventually sold the cribs across the street, but continued to live in her Front Street house in Salida. She rented the rooms to the working railroad men and spent her leisure time still taking money. Now it was money bet on card games, which was a nightly ritual Laura and her railroad boarders thoroughly enjoyed.

Laura died in 1953, at her Salida home she had loved for nearly fifty years. She went quietly and perhaps even peacefully. Her well attended funeral took place on a cold snowy April day, with burial in the quiet Salida cemetery.[12]

Yet, true to the end, she died as she had lived; on her terms.

◊ LILLIAN POWERS WAS ONE OF the few madams to begin her career as one of the "girls." At least *she* admitted it. Anyway, "Lil" as she soon became known, chose her profession quite willingly.

Lillian Powers is thought to have been born in a small farming community in Wisconsin. Her parents were Swedish immigrants just settling in a new country. As a teenager, Lillian taught in a one-room school house, but hated it. Young and full of determination, she left home at the age of sixteen. She worked as a laundress in another small town and soon became the best producer in the establishment, earning her the nickname "Laundry Queen." A short time later, Lil changed her profession, which changed her life, and as she said in an interview shortly before her death, "I have no regrets."[13]

Lil seems to have been content in her working profession. Yet, she had a goal. She wanted to move west, where gold had been discovered and she wanted to be a part of the new excitement. In a mining town in South Dakota, Lil heard of the great gold strike at Cripple Creek, Colorado. With all her belongings and considerable savings, Lil headed for Colorado. She stopped for a short time in Denver, not long after the *House of Mirrors* had opened. She rented a crib on Market Street, but soon found the girls were cutting prices to attract more clientele. Lil couldn't make money that way. Next, she tried the Alcazar Theatre, a noted dance hall, at Twentieth and Market Streets. Working as a dance hall girl didn't sit well with Lil. The girls, Lil included, were on their feet the entire night, entertaining, serving drinks, and dancing with the paying customers. For this, each girl received fifty cents a night! No tips, no percentage of bar receipts, just fifty cents a night. One night was enough for Lil. She knew she could make better money.

Lil acquired a crib on Market Street, not far from one of Mattie Silk's parlor houses. Lil met Mattie Silks when two men who were customers of hers, came to the crib one night wanting to go to Mattie place. The men wanted Lil to go with them, so they would be more comfortable. Lil said she would have to be paid. The two customers paid Lil ten dollars each. She said in an interview years later that she was so excited, she practically had to drag the two customers to Mattie's. Lil's customers were the perfect gentlemen at Mattie's parlor house, and paid cash for all their requirements. Mattie, who was observing the trio, introduced herself. Lil said Mattie was very kind and after learning of Lil's profession, the two became good friends.

Lil left Denver shortly after the incident for the rich gold mining camp of Cripple Creek, which was a bustling, busy, booming little town when she arrived.

There were no openings at any of the many parlor houses on Myers Avenue, or in the crib district of Poverty Gulch, for that matter. So Lil went over the mountain to the south, to Victor.

While Victor was in the Cripple Creek Mining District, there were plenty of mines, and mining business was a bit slower than in Cripple Creek. Lil found work right away and saved as much as she could. As soon as she heard of an opening in Cripple Creek, she left Victor.

In Cripple Creek, she rented a crib in upper Poverty Gulch,(even cribs had a social status of their own,) from the town's legendary prostitute Leo the Lion.

When Lil arrived, she didn't open her door for business right away, as most of the soiled doves did. Instead, she got buckets of water, soap, and rags and cleaned her new "establishment." Then she decorated. Oh, nothing fancy, but she did have dainty curtains and pillows. Her place was neat and tidy. And most important to Lil, it was clean. Her sheets were changed and cleaned regularly.

"I made good right away," she said. She made just as much money from beer sales and tips as she did from sex. Lil did a great business in Cripple Creek, even if it was just a crib and despite her many run-ins with an ever-drunk Leo the Lion. Leo became increasingly upset at Lil's growing business and felt Lil was stealing customers from her. The drunken cat fights and shouting matches increased.

One mid-morning, a very drunk Leo the Lion stormed into Lil's crib, shouting and cussing. She told Lil she was stealing business, called her a few names, and told her to get out. Leo's ranting and raving went on and eventually she pulled a gun. She threatened to shoot Lil if she wasn't gone by nightfall. For the first time, Lil was actually afraid of Leo the Lion.

"Oh, she was a meaner." Lil remembered. " I told her I'd get out. I was young, I knew I could make it. I was out of luck now, though."[14]

Eventually, Leo the Lion wandered back to her crib, and Lil sprang into action. She ran all the way to the telephone office and asked the operator to connect her to Miss Laura Evans in Salida. After an anxious few minutes, the call was put through and Lil made employment arrangements with Laura. Rushing back to her crib, she hired a boy to help her pack and clean, Lil would not leave an unkept crib behind, even if Leo the Lion didn't deserve it. With the crib cleaned and Lil's belongings packed, she made her way, with the help of the hired boy, up the steep hill to the railroad depot. Lil looked through the window at Cripple Creek for the last time, as the train pulled out of town and the eastern sunrise broke through the pre-dawn haze.

Years later, thinking back on that time, Lillian Powers said in an interview, "Oh, but that Leo the Lion, she was a tough one."

Late in the evening, the train pulled in at Salida. Lil eventually found her way to Laura Evans' two story parlor house. After introducing herself to Laura she offered the rent up front for the crib across the street and two days back rent (from the original phone call.) Laura took the rent, but refused the back rent. This encounter endeared the women to each other, a friendship that would last more than forty years.

At Salida, Lil continued her routine, with the same business results. First she cleaned her cribs from top to bottom, then decorated, and finally she opened for business. In time her customer base built up and Lil made good money. Miss Laura took notice and offered her a room in her parlor house across the street. Lil politely declined, stating she liked her own place and felt she could make more money. Laura soon agreed and eventually turned the entire crib row over to Lil for a percentage of the earnings. Lil knew her business.

After several years in Salida, Lil had saved considerable money and felt the time had come to open her own parlor house. Lil was ready to join the great madams of Colorado. She said goodbye to Laura Evans. They would visit each other often in the years to come.

Lil left town by train with all her belongings once again. This time she headed for Florence, a small railroad town not far from Canon City. She bought a large building at the south end of the town, near the railroad tracks. It was shortly after World War I and with the GIs coming home, Lil knew her timing was right. She employed just a few girls.

"You know, if you have a bunch of girls and don't make very much money, you're losing money.," Lil said. "It's the nature of the business, ya know. So that's the trouble."

Lil spent a good amount of time and money improving her new place before she opened for business. There was a large open area that became an outdoor beer garden, with a dance floor and live music. She renovated the inside for the winter months by building a ballroom. There was a large sitting room with fine furnishings and dainty pillows, Lil's style, of course. The rest of the floor included the formal dining room, a roomy kitchen, and Lil's private room. At the front of the long hall, near the ballroom, a stairway conveniently led upstairs to the "pleasure rooms."

Lil's new business was an immediate success. The locals flocked to her establishment. When word got out about Lil's place, railroaders who had known her in Salida now stopped in Florence. Everyone knew *Lil's Place* and so the name stuck. Somehow, she also picked up the name "Tiger Lil."

No one in Florence today seems to know how the name came about, but the town historian, Darryl Lindsey, says "Everyone here in Florence knew her by that name." And he should know, because he personally knew Lil when he was just a kid. Lindsey described how she bounced back after the various reform movements came and went. And of how well her business did during and after World War II, when the boys at Fort Carson came to Florence and *Lil's Place* on their Liberty Passes.

However, reform finally won out in 1949. Fremont County district attorney John Stump Witcher was forced to close down Lil's Place, and she was forced to send her girls away. She lived for another ten years alone in the place she had built and made successful. She had boarders from time to time, but Lil preferred to live alone. She didn't go out much. Darryl Lindsey sometimes drove her home after an afternoon at the local grocery store would see her at the post office. He said she was a kindly lady and would invite him in to see her place.

The local papers record Lil's hospital stay in February 1960. Shortly after that, she was moved to a nursing home, where her health began to decline. Yet, true to her nature, Lil got her affairs in order. She had sold her property in Florence made out her will, and told her local friends of her last wishes. Lil died quietly in October of 1960. She was the last of the great Colorado madams.

When Lillian Powers died in 1960, a century-long era in Colorado history also died.

———————❦———————

End Notes: Chapter Three

1   Fred Mazzulla files, Colorado Historical Society.

2   Author, *The Wildest of the West.*

3   Miami County court records and 1850 and 1860 census

4   Descendants of the family are still prominent in Denver today, thus the family name will remain unnamed by this author.

5   Many historians have spelled Laura's name *Evens,* as spelled on her tombstone. All recorded legal documents with signatures that I have seen have the spelling, *Evans.* Chaffee County historian June Shaputis surmises the tombstone spelling is an error on the part of the funeral directors.

6   Miller and Mazulla, *Holladay Street*

7   One of the original brass checks is in the possession of June Shaputis, Chaffee County historian.

8   Miller and Mazulla, *Holladay Street*

9   Bancroft, *Six Racy Madams,* page 40.

10   For the full story of Jack the Ripper, see Chapter 5.

11   Miller and Mazulla, *Holladay Street.*

12   Her tombstone incorrectly gives the spelling as Evens.

13   The Mazzulla files, Colorado Historical Society.

14   Miller, *Holladay Street.*

FOUR

My God! Isn't this awful?
— Coroner McHatton

Tenderloin Tragedies

ragedies occurred with great regularity in the tenderloin districts of Colorado. The very nature of these women who escaped from their past, eluded the truth, and lived under false pretenses lent themselves to a life of tragedy. The less than ideal lifestyle left many a soiled dove lonely and depressed. The living conditions were often cramped, dark and dirty. Any one of these conditions could lead to a sad circumstance. A combination often led to tragic endings. Tragedies that came in any number of ways.

A portrait of sadness hangs in the Cripple Creek Old Homestead parlor museum.

The streets of Colorado City were alive with the hustle and bustle of a boom town. A supply town along Fountain Creek, in 1859, Colorado City served the gold mining area of the South Park region. The town did well for awhile, but it was about thirty years too early for the real gold rush in the area. Within ten years the town would be almost deserted. Yet, during that decade, the folks in Colorado City lived life to the fullest.

The town was doing so well in the beginning, and with prominence in the offing, the city council felt confident enough to bid for the 1862 nomination for capital of the Colorado Territory, which ultimately went to Denver. In those formidable years, the citizens of Colorado City prided themselves in being an "open" town, selling liquor and espousing the "entertainment for life." There were several saloons and gambling establishments, and there was the tenderloin district along Washington Avenue.

The popular house of ill repute was known as *The Mansion*, owned by Mayme Majors. Miss Lucille Deming was also a favorite of the row. Others included Bell Bristol, Hazy Maizie, Dolly Worling, Minnie Davenport, the beloved Laura Bell McDaniel, and later, retired madam Blanche Burton, who called Colorado City home. Laura Bell had a bordello near the *Crystal Palace*, where Bob Ford, killer of Jesse James, spent considerable time playing cards. Today, Laura Bell's place operates as a nursing home. Minnie Smith was the envy of many of the soiled doves. She owned a brightly painted buggy pulled by a fine set of horses, and was often seen driving through town.

The main red light district was located in the area bounded by Colorado Avenue, 26th Street, and Cucharras Street. More than twenty saloons operated in this square block area. The majority of the establishments had second floor dance halls and many had alley exits that allowed customers discreet access to the Cucharras Street bordellos. It is said tunnels once existed connecting the legal saloons of Colorado Avenue to the illegal red light operations of Cucharras Street. Today, Madam Mamie Rogers' brothel at 2616 W. Cucharras, is a private residence, however it may still retain a portion of the infamous tunnels.

Blanche Burton's grave in the Colorado City cemetery, says simply, "Pioneer Madam."

Blanche Burton is thought to be the first madam of the great Cripple Creek gold camps. It is said her reputation as a madam was second only to Hazel Vernon and the infamous Pearl DeVere.

By the turn of the century, Blanche had made Colorado City her home. She was known in the community for her charitable donations and volunteer work for the poor. Her life came to a tragic and mysterious end in 1909. According to newspaper accounts, Blanche was in her home on Colorado Avenue when a curtain caught fire from a knocked-over oil lamp. Splattered with oil and her clothing burning, Blanche ran from the house. Two policemen met her, throwing coats and snow on her. Hours later she was dead.

According to witnesses, a man was seen running from the scene. The police were unable to link the man to the crime.

In her many acts of kindness, just the day before she died, Blanche had spent the last of her money for the month on a ton of coal, much of which she gave away, another act of her generosity. Her obituary stated in part:

> . . . *Blanche Burton was a good nurse, ever ready to respond when anyone was sick or in distress.*[1]

Blanche was buried on a cold, snowy Christmas Eve, with the services paid for by a fellow madam. Her grave was unmarked.

In 1983, a local club raised money to erect a marker. The granite stone memorializing Blanche says, "Pioneer Madam."[2]

Sophie was a young, pretty blond prostitute on Denver's Market Street, who, like many others of her chosen profession, had fallen in love with one of her customers. Her lover was a college student who gave Sophie his fraternity pin as a token of his devotion. The two became inseparable. When the young man gave Sophie a diamond engagement ring, they made plans for the future. When the parents of the boy were told of the engagement, they were less than thrilled. The young couple's dream was about to change forever.

The father made a large monetary offer to Sophie if she would break off the engagement and never see his son again. Sophie refused. The father was desperate. Soon World War I erupted in Europe. The young man wanted to enlist, but hesitated because of Sophie. At last, the parents found their answer to separate Sophie and the young man. They encouraged the son to join the Army, with a trite promise: following the war, should he still wish to marry Sophie, they would have no objections.

With that promise, the young man said goodbye to Sophie with his own promises of the future. A forlorn Sophie wrote to her beloved regularly, and followed the war news faithfully through the local papers for more than two years.

Reading the Denver papers one spring day in 1918, Sophie went into shock. Her beloved fiancé was listed among those recently killed in action. Distraught and alone, with the promise of a normal life gone, Sophie swallowed poison and died.

Dottie Watson, a Silverton madam became a ward of the court in May 1900. The particulars of her case are difficult to decipher; however, the local papers reveal Dottie was found insane by a Silverton court and removed to the Colorado insane asylum at Pueblo.

Ed Harless was a successful Victor businessman when his wife disappeared shortly after the Thanksgiving holiday in 1902. The couple were known to have had "marital problems." However, Victorian manners being as they were, the social circle of Victor looked the other way.

In any case, Ed Harless left Victor in search of his wife. During a brief stay in Denver, Harless paid a call on a clairvoyant who said his wife could be found in Silverton. Harless arrived in Silverton the following day, and went to Marshal Leonard with his information. The following day, the marshal had found Mrs. Harless, and took Ed to see her that afternoon. The husband was in shock and disbelief as the marshal led him down the walk of the notorious Blair Street. The men entered a small bordello, and walked into a dark room. The marshal spoke to the lady crouched in a chair and walked to the window. Pulling the shade open, he turned as Mrs. Harless screamed. He saw Ed Harless pointing a revolver at his wife. He lunged at Harless and managed to get the gun away.

The marshal took Harless to jail, where he was charged with a misdemeanor, paid the fine and was released.[3] Victor business directories showed Ed Harless back in Victor until 1905, after which, his name disappears. What happened to Mrs. Harless is not known.

In 1886, young Annie Blythe married the man of her dreams, Sam Seas, a railroad worker, in Boulder. Annie's upscale parents were less than pleased and so Sam took his new bride to Como, where he took a job at the South Park rail center. Times were happy for the couple in Como until each of their three children died in infancy. Annie sank into severe depression and began to drink heavily. On the night of April 6, 1894, while Sam was on an extended freight train run to Climax, Annie attended a party where the town marshal was shot and killed.

The murderer was arrested. Annie was charged as an accessory to the crime. Sam hired an attorney for his wife and Annie was acquitted. Sam divorced Annie soon after the trial. Desperate, Annie left Como for Denver, where she found work in the crib area of Market Street. Annie's mother came from Boulder to Denver on a couple of occasions to intervene in her daughter's behavior, but was unsuc-cessful.

On July 5, 1898, Annie was found brutally beaten by one of her many cus-tomers or boyfriends. She died the next day. The official autopsy report listed the cause of death as severe alcoholism. The boyfriend was never questioned.

And Annie's mother made one more final trip to Denver for her daughter.

Mystery seems to be a common thread in the lives of many of our tenderloin ladies. None more so than the life of Lois Lovell. Lois worked in one of the many houses of ill repute on Denver's Market Street.

She had been seeing a certain customer on a more than regular basis, and the two eventually fell in love. The businessman proposed marriage, to which a touched Lois replied for all its drama, "No, darling, I won't marry you because I love you."

After several attempts to convince Lois to change her mind, her suitor left town on a business trip. It is said as the train rolled out of town and the whistle echoed against the front range of the Rocky Mountains, Lois swallowed poison and died.

When the young businessman returned, he had new ideas to sway Lois into marriage. When he inquired after Lois at the Market Street address, he was told of her death. Stunned, he asked directions to her resting place. At her gravesite, he seemed to grieve a bit before putting a pistol to his head. His dead body fell upon the fresh dug grave of Lois Lovell, where he was later interred beside her.

Historians have often written of Lois Lovell's relation to Lillis Lovell, discussed in a previous chapter. Many contend Lois and Lillis were sisters. At first glance, an assumption could be made. According to death certificates for both Lois and Lillis, their true birth surname was Quigley. However, further research suggests they were not sisters. Lillis Lovell's will, quite extensive, and a bit cold hearted considering her wealth, shows an unhappy family situation. Yet, it also shows a family lineage which, carefully checked, leaves little doubt that the two were *not* related. In her will, Lillis leaves one dollar to her *only sister, Mrs. Mary Nirene Quigley Wilder*, who also happened to live in Denver. The fact that Lois Lovell was not married at the time of Lillis' death, given her refusal of marriage, lends credence to the single sister status. No marriage certificate for Lois exists in county court records searched for the years of 1900 to 1908. Of course there could have been a secret marriage. If so, it would have been the real underlying reason Lois later poisoned herself.

Mysterious indeed.

❧ Another madam mystery is the story of Denver's first lady of the tenderloin. Her story starts off as many of those early pioneers now known in Colorado as the 59er's. A young Midwestern teenager, Ada married a promising, budding young minister in a blessed union that all in attendance were sure would last the test of time. Soon the cry "Pikes Peak or Bust" swelled across the land. Like thousands of Easterners heading west on little more than a hope and a prayer, the newlyweds packed a wagon and joined the westward migration.

Nineteen year old Ada La Mont arrived at the Cherry Creek gold diggings in late 1858 or the spring of 1859 — alone.

Overland wagon trains took weeks, even months to cross the wind-swept prairie west to the Rocky Mountains. In their book, *The 59er's*, authors Zamonski and Keller relate the story of a mysterious disappearance. One evening Ada's husband, the young minister disappeared. Finding no trace of him and with the fear of an Indian attack, the wagon train halted for a day and a search party was organized. Meanwhile, it was discovered a young woman of questionable background also was missing. When the search party returned empty-handed, it was generally believed the two had willingly left the wagon train.

As the wagon train resumed its westward journey, a silent, brooding Ada La Mont contemplated her life and her future. When the wagon train reached the struggling settlement of Denver City, complete with an Indian camp on the eastern edge, Ada reportedly announced:

As a God fearing woman, you see me for the last time. As of tomorrow, I start the first brothel in this settlement. Any of you men in need of a little fun will always find the flaps of my tent open.

Ada was a striking dark haired beauty and her sensational debut in infant Denver guaranteed her success. Within a year, business was thriving and she opened the first parlor house in Denver, on Arapahoe Street, the newest part of town, and the first high class house of ill-repute. She served quality liquor, when she could get it, and her house and her girls were clean and well groomed.

For ten years, Ada reigned supreme in Denver's tenderloin world. She even had a long term intimate relationship with a popular gambling proprietor, the dashing and mysterious Charley Harrison.

Yet, Ada's life took a sudden and fateful turn for the worse. A friend of Ada's happened across a human skull on the eastern plains, on a return trip from Kansas.

The skull had a large hole in the back and a spent bullet lodged in the bone. Rotting clothing found nearby held a Bible, with the inscription written by Ada to her minister husband. When presented with the news and the inscribed Bible, Ada went into seclusion. She began to drink. She lost interest in herself and her business. Eventually, Ada left Denver. A short time later, she showed up in Georgetown. Nothing halted Ada's downward spiral. She died in poverty in a single room shack. Even her funeral was unattended.

꧁ Fire was a constant concern in Colorado's frontier days, and rightly so. Most buildings were built from wood. Inside, heat was provided by wood or coal burning stoves, while light was provided by oil lamps and candles. It is no wonder there were so many fires in Colorado's early years. Fires devastated towns and nearly wiped out others. Fire was the cause of many tenderloin tragedies.

In Silverton, when a coal lamp exploded in Mabel Pierce's bordello on Blair Street, Miss Marble, as she was known, along with her girls, rushed to connect a hose to their water reservoir and quickly extinguished the flames. The local paper reported no loss of life and minor damage.

Clara Smith died in Denver's tenderloin district when her ball gown caught fire from a stove. Her sad funeral, covered by the local papers, took place in a back room of the coroner's office.

August 21, 1899 will forever be a changing day in the history of Victor. Fire was sparked at either Rosa May's dance hall, the 999, or Lilly Ried's small bordello, both located between 3rd and 4th Streets. The fire spread to some fourteen blocks and caused an estimated one million dollars in damage. The following day, the folks of Victor picked up, cleared out the destruction and began to build, in brick.

Shortly after midnight on May 1, 1883, flames lit up the night sky over Leadville's tenderloin district. H. A. W. Tabor's elite fire brigade rushed to the scene. Concern soon turned to panic as several soiled doves ran out of the houses in screaming fright. Mabel Holman's house (leased from Sallie Purple) was completely destroyed, but all the girls were safe. Mattie White lost her house and one girl was slightly injured. Water damage put Mollie May out of business for a few days, but no one was hurt. The origin of the fire was in Georgie Dunbar's second floor room in Mabel Holman's house. How it started remains a mystery. The total damage to the three bordellos was more than $12,000.

Tragedy also struck on Georgetown's Brownell Street. When fire swept through the area, Jennie Aiken died in the raging fire of her parlor house.

Fire ravaged the tenderloin of Colorado City in 1909. Several bordellos on Cucharras Street were destroyed. The girls of the area were still reeling from the devastation when two days later, fire blazed through once again. This fire, which was followed by a third, caused severe damage beyond the row. But the red light girls soon bounced back. Headed by veteran madam Laura Bell McDaniel, the bordellos of Colorado City rose again. Laura Bell built an enormous house and life in Colorado City's tenderloin went on.[4]

In Durango, a tenderloin tragedy occurred with the burning death of Julia Wheeler. A fire started in her bordello around midnight on a Friday night. *The Durango Herald* reported on May 14, 1889: ". . . the sporting woman was burned . . . the piano and most of the furniture, however were saved."

Mayme Murphy had worked in Silverton's tenderloin district for many years. In her older age (just past forty) she rented a crib. Because of her her cranky way of addressing children, Mayme became known as the "old lady" in Silverton. Rheumatism plagued Mayme in later years. One evening, she plugged in her electric heating pad and electrocuted herself.[5] Mayme Murphy was buried unceremoniously in the local graveyard.

❧ AMY BASSETT IS ANOTHER OF our ladies who sheltered her past. Historians have their theories, but none agree. It is said that Amy came to Denver from Kentucky, or Ohio, or Kansas City. She is said to have led an immoral life and therefore was forced from the family into a life of sin. Or she is thought to have married into a political family, shamed them, and then was exiled. And, it is said she had a young son back East, who had no idea of his mother's true identity, or she had two older sons, both college graduates. Take your pick.

In any case, Amy Bassett arrived in Denver in 1888 and soon found employment at one of Jennie Rogers' houses at 2015 Market Street. Eventually, she leased the house from Jennie and ran her own business — quite well by most accounts. Her "pleasure resort" was included in the advertisements of Denver's 1892 *Red Book*, the pocket-sized guide intended for Denver's elite businessman.

Tragedy came January 1, 1904 when Amy, cleaning her clothes with gasoline, was overcome with fumes. An explosion occurred and Amy, trapped in the room, was overcome by smoke and flames. Policemen finally found her and rushed her out of the building and to the hospital. Amy Bassett died the next day from lung collapse and severe burns. She was thirty-four years old. Her funeral, held at the new stately Fairmount Cemetery, was attended by Denver's demimonde. The city had never expected such a spectacle at their new *modern* cemetery. The press had a field day:

> Amy Bassett reigned a veritable queen of (the) Street. Many were the conquests she made, and the homes she wrecked . . . on several occasions she was implicated in brawls and was seriously injured, marring most of her noted beauty. — The Rocky Mountain News, January 2, 1904

🖎 Sickness was also a cause of death among our tenderloin ladies. Health has always been an issue in Colorado. Many Easterners came to the Rocky Mountain region for health concerns, rather than gold or silver. Generally called consumptives in the days before modern medicine, Colorado's climate eased those who suffered from many respiratory ailments, including asthma and tuberculosis. However, Colorado's high climate also could pose a real danger.

Pneumonia was probably the number one cause of natural deaths, given the high, cold winter climate. Crude and unsanitary living conditions were a contributing factor, if not a direct cause for much of the sickness. Dysentery, scurvy and bowel ailments were common. Other diseases were contagious and could effect, or infect, an entire town. Diphtheria, influenza, scarlet fever, and small pox all claimed many lives in early Colorado.

Pneumonia, in particular, claimed many victims across Colorado, and the soiled doves were not immune. The following story was best told by the *Cripple Creek Morning Times* of January 21, 1896:

> One of the saddest scenes that has occurred in the camp for some time was witnessed last night in a little room over Mernie's Dance Hall. It was a death bed scene and the surroundings made it affecting. On a bed in a dingy room lay a woman, an unfortunate woman. Around her bed stood other unfortunate women who shed tears and administered to the woman's wants as well as their untrained hands could do. The sick woman was young, only nineteen years old, and exceedingly handsome, but the dreaded disease of pneumonia had driven her to bed and was slowly but surely closing her lungs and making each breath more difficult. Only a week ago, the same woman had been on the floor below as merry as anyone there . . . on the same floor, while her life was ebbing, the caller was yelling

out in his usual loud manner, and the shuffle of the feet of the dancers could be heard. The sick woman realized she was about to die and asked for a drink of water. Just as her attendant reached for the pitcher, the caller on the floor below called out, "Promenade to the bar!" The sick woman's muscles relaxed, her head lay motionless on the pillow, and she was dead. The music in the dance hall below was dismissed, the lights turned out, and the undertaker's wagon bore the remains of Ruth Davenport off to the cooling room.

Pneumonia also took a good many of Silverton's population in the winter of 1900-1901. The town's soiled doves were not immune:

On February 2, 1901, at 3 o'clock Wednesday morning, from a life that was black to the blind, "Madge," one of the girls employed at Luke's Dance Hall, crossed the channel of death into the vale of mystery. The disease was pneumonia and the burial occurred from Prosser's undertaking establishment at 3 o'clock Thursday afternoon.

— — —

On May 25, 1901, Ella Keeton, a poor unfortunate who operated at Luke's Dance Hall for the past six weeks, died on Wednesday morning at about 11 o'clock. The woman was about forty years old and the disease which removed her from the glitter of dance hall life, was pneumonia. Subscription was raised among the sporting fraternity sufficient to defray the expense of burial. Rev. George Eaves made a good talk at the funeral which occurred from Prosser's Undertaking Room Thursday afternoon at 2 o'clock.[6]

A tragic life came to a sad end for a Leadville soiled dove. Anna Brock, a young teenager from an Indiana farming family, ran off at the age of nineteen with a drummer in a band from St. Louis, Missouri. The two wed in St. Louis, yet little else is known of her past, before she arrived in Leadville in February 1882. In Leadville, she took the name Nellie Bartlett and found work at one of the dance halls. Nellie was warm and friendly, and made many friends in her new sisterhood of soiled doves.

Shortly after the New Year celebration of 1883, Nellie became very ill. Doctors came and went; nothing could be done for her. Her friends cleaned an empty cabin at the end of State Street and moved her there. A friend or two always stayed with her, but the end came on February 25, 1883. Her friends said she was twenty-two years old.

The girls also told reporters that 'Anna Brock' was her true maiden name and that her marriage certificate was among her belongings. Anna had also made a last request — to let her hometown know that 'Anna Brock was dead.' "That will be enough," she said. To the end, she spared her family from her chosen lifestyle.

That afternoon, as a rosewood casket with the body of Anna Brock was carried out of the log cabin, her frail sisters told the reporter of the *Leadville Evening Chronicle*:

> *Yesterday morning in a little log cabin . . . there was general sorrow. Along one side of the little room on a snow white pallet was lain the lifeless form of poor Anna Brock. Flowers... were strewn about her pillow, and by strange hands woven into her hair. 'Please don't put a bad piece in the paper about poor Anna,' said one of the several female mourners to the reporter as he was taking his leave of the room of death. 'Don't say another unfortunate, a soiled sister, fair creature. Don't make fun of her in the paper, nor speak of her as if she had not been a human being. If she was a low dance girl she was good and we all loved her, and we are going to give her a Christian funeral. We girls have put up two hundred dollars to pay for a respectable burial.' This remark was seconded by all the dance girls in the room and there were no others.*

DEATH WITH A DIMES WORTH

Many members of Colorado's demimonde used alcohol and drugs to dull their unhappy existence. Drug preparations in many forms were available for sale at any local drug store. From a dime to a quarter, small bottles of morphine, cocaine, laudanum, and many other potions were enough to end a tortured life. Morphine, cocaine, and laudanum were used to escape the misery. Laudanum, a derivative of opium, could be purchased at the local pharmacy, and so became the wonder drug of choice. Taken in liquid form, it soothed the common headache, eased aches and pains, and tended to make one feel happier or more at ease. It was also addictive and deadly. Carbolic acid was widely used as a douche when diluted, but was also a means of suicide. This often led to a wayward, sliding lifestyle, leading to violence or death.

Viola was such a case. Her sad, empty life came to an alcoholic end in Central City. She was thirty-three years old. Viola had a husband and children in the life

This photo shows Bob Ford's girls in his Creede bordello. The killer of Jessie James, Ford showed a tender side when he paid the funeral expenses of one of his girls.

Amy Bassett, shown in a post mortem state, is representative of many a sad tale of the soiled dove.

Tenderloin tragedies were constant, and death was common. Typical soiled doves funerals were small and unceremonious, unlike that of Miss Laura Evans who lived a long colorful life.

Denver Public Library

Suicide was an unfortunate fact of life in the Tenderloin districts. Death happened quickly for some, as the victim seems to be holding the bottle of her "magic potion."

Old Homestead Museum

Hopeful, even happy, were the lives of a few soiled doves.

The bedrooms of the *Old Homestead* parlor house in Cripple Creek were furnished in high quality, an example of the detail Madam Pearl DeVere displayed throughout her house.

Kathy Kriss collection

Cripple Creek citizens buried their beloved Pearl DeVere, the largest funeral in Cripple Creek, and later replaced her headstone with this loving tribute. -credit author's collection

Several such medications became sources for suicide

Colorado Historical Society

The original door of the back entrance of the *Old Homestead*, was found in the basement, years after Pearl's death. The shipping address was to *"Isabelle Martin."* Mystery followed the beloved Cripple Creek madam even after her death.

she left behind. An adulterous affair left her shattered, alone and desperate. Viola left everything behind for the mining towns of the Rockies. In Central City she made her living as a prostitute in the high gulch area, yet her unhealthy living conditions and terrible loneliness caused her desire for the bottle. Following her death, the *Weekly-Register Call* reported her funeral rather straight forward: ". . . deposited in a narrow grave in Potter's Field, in the bleak mountains of Gilpin County."[7]

The *Rocky Mountain News* chose to show its tender side with regard to the soiled doves, in the following obituary of sorts:

As the Rev. G.A. Schmidt, Twenty-sixth and Lawrence streets, read the impressive ritual for the dead and then offered a short prayer; the members of his audience stirred uneasily and looked fixedly ahead. They sat quietly afterward during the pause that ensued before the coffin was carried out. Then quickly and with sighs of relief they hurried out.

The new plot out at Riverside will be marked by a plain slab bearing the name "Clara Smith" and the dates of her death. That is not her right name. What her name really was, who her parents were and where they lived, are things not known, in the underworld no one knew. There she was simply Clara Smith.

Somewhere a mother and father, possibly as old and feeble as the old charwoman who placed the wreath on the coffin, will mourn for a lost daughter. To them she will be missed only. Of her death they probably will never hear. That her funeral was attended by no one save the scarlet women, the expenses met by their subscriptions and the service held in the rear room of a coroner's office, they will never know. That much is spared them. — The Rocky Mountain News, October 5, 1912

Nellie Russell, a native of St. Joseph, Missouri, arrived in Creede in June 1892. A pretty young girl, she was hired by Bob Ford to join his "ladies of the evening." A day later, she was found dead, the result of alcohol poisoning and morphine overdose. Bob Ford paid for her burial, signing the note with this epitaph:

Charity covereth a multitude of sins.

A profound epitaph with double meaning, for minutes after Ford signed for Miss Russell's funeral expenses, he was murdered by Ed O. Kelly.

Lulu Slain, another soiled dove working in Upper Creede, died of an overdose of morphine and was buried in an unmarked grave in the new Creede cemetery.

Carbolic acid was used in the suicide of Lucy Phillips, a twenty-four-year-old prostitute of Victor, who had a history of attempted suicides. Fay Anderson also ended her life by carbolic acid. The Salida newspaper reported she worked for Ida Brooks' G Street house, and died after "hours of agony."

Mattie Silks, the famous Denver madam, was deeply saddened when a tragic event happened in one of her bordellos in 1892. Two of Mattie's girls, Allie Ellis and Effie Pryor, began an evening drinking away their problems and ended the following day near death. Depressed over an ended love affair, Allie poured her troubles out to Effie, as the two drank all night long. Evidently, according to the Denver newspapers, sometime toward morning, the two soiled doves took morphine. Later in the morning, Mattie discovered the girls, near death, but alive. Both were ". . . lying on their backs, disrobed and gasping for breath." A doctor was summoned, and he immediately pumped the stomachs of both girls. Effie lived, but Allie died a few days later.

> West Holladay Street was this afternoon the scene of a suicide which threw the inhabitants of that part of the city into a frenzy of excitement and caused nearly all the women in the neighborhood to energy from the humble tenements which line the greater thoroughfare, and stand, bareheaded, with arms akimbo about the waist. There in a small room, black with smoke of ages and the air which was overpoweringly unpleasant, lay stretched on a dirt bed, a woman, dead. Her name was Mrs. Winger . . . she had been drinking heavily and swallowed a dose of morphine. On the bed beside the dead woman, lay a terrier, her pet, whining piteously. The remains were taken away for inquest and the dog followed the undertaker's wagon. —The Denver Times, December 15, 1886

Hidden by false pasts and invented names, very few prostitutes actually escaped their past or the reason, whatever it may have been, for their current situation and way of life. The sad evidence of this is the high number of suicides. In Cripple Creek, the following report appeared in the local paper:

> Nellie Rolfe, a woman of the half world, was found dead in her room at 377 Myers Avenue at about 4 o'clock yesterday afternoon by a woman living near the home of the deceased. The cause of death is not known, and whether or not the

woman committed suicide is a question. When found, the woman was in a crouched position on the floor leaning against the bed with her head resting on her arm. She had in all probability been dead for several hours, as the muscles were tightly drawn. The remains were taken charge of by Beil and Gersell, undertakers. The woman was a victim to the morphine habit. Three small bottles of the drug and two hypodermic syringes were found on the dresser of her room." — *Cripple Creek Times*, January 3, 1903

Annie James had been in Silverton for over a year. She worked at Ludwig Vota's dance hall. The ladies of Blair Street said she was kind and good hearted. Despite her outward appearance, Annie must have been very sad and lonely. In April of 1897, Annie swallowed a bottle of carbolic acid. Her friends in the dance hall discovered her condition late in the evening, and alerting a doctor, everything was done to save her life. Just before midnight, the doctor pronounced her dead, as her friends wept by her bedside. It was then discovered that Annie had left a note. Signed by Annie, the note said simply: "I can't stand your abuse any longer, good bye." It is thought a love affair gone bad was the reason for the suicide.

One of Creede's soiled doves, Timberline Rose Vastine, was popular in the mining camp. Her height of over six feet, two inches, obviously accounts for her name. One cold evening, Timberline climbed up into the hills above Creede and shot herself not once, but reportedly six times. Amazingly, she lived, but what became of her is lost to history.

In Durango, a young, desperate prostitute committed suicide with an extreme amount of morphine. A sad occurrence that happened all too often. However, for reasons unexplained, a prostitute's funeral was a major affair in Durango. A horse-drawn hearse was followed by several buggies and carriages filled with the girls from the red light district. The entourage made the long trip to the Animas City Cemetery, or in later years, the stately Greenmount Cemetery. The attending band, it was always a band, played soft, mournful music as the gravesite ceremonies proceeded. The many flower arrangements from the church service were placed lovingly at the grave, as the mourners said a silent farewell.

Mary Gover committed suicide with an overdose of morphine. Her sad circumstance was best described by the *Rocky Mountain News* of May 6, 1896:

Mrs. Mary Gover, who lived upstairs at 2025 Curtis Street until she died there at 10 o'clock this morning, bought 25 cents worth of morphine in a drug store at

Nineteenth and Curtis streets at 11 o'clock last night. A few moments later she walked into the Buckeye saloon at 2031 Curtis Street.

"Hello Charlie," she said to proprietor Walbrecht of the place; "I'm going to kill my self."

"What for?" queried the saloon keeper in some surprise.

"Too poor to live," the woman answered.

IN THE EARLY SUNRISE OF a new day, Ella Wellington retired to her posh bedroom on the upper floor of 1942 Market Street, after a glorious all night gala, resplendent in silk and jewels. Softly she whispered, "I'm oh so happy," as she put a pistol to her head and died in her blood soaked finery.

No one knew much about Ella Wellington when she arrived in Denver in 1889. She opened her own business operation on Market Street, Denver's row. In time she became associated with, as well as a friend, to both Mattie Silks and Jennie Rogers. In fact, court records show Ella paid a down payment to Jennie Rogers and signed a two year note for the purchase of Jenny's famous *House of Mirrors* at 1942 Market Street.[8]

It was also at this time that Ella began a friendship with the deputy clerk of the Denver courts, William Prinn. Although Prinn was a married man, he and Ella soon shared an intimate relationship.

For a time, all seemed well in Ella's world. Her establishment was listed in Denver's 1892 *Red Book* as "Everything First-Class." Her clientele were some of the wealthiest of Denver's business leaders.

Yet, Ella's personal life was far from happy. She was prone to fits of melancholy and more than once attempted suicide. Over time she revealed her past to only a few close friends. Her real name was Ella Brouse, a divorced woman who had left her home in Omaha, as well as her two adopted children, with a man named Sam Cross. The two spent time in Salt Lake City before Ella came to Denver, alone.

On the evening of Thursday, July 26, 1894, Ella and her girls held a formal party complete with the finest foods, wine, music, and dance. The gala lasted into the early morning hours. Guests arrived at all hours and were greeted warmly by the hostess. None more so than a group of businessmen from Omaha who arrived around midnight. One of the men in the Omaha group was an old friend of Ella's and her ex-husband's.

The two spent the remainder of the early morning hours reminiscing, as the wine flowed and the sun began to rise. Inquiring as to the state of her adopted children, her old friend assured her they were well cared for and very happy. The friend went on to give an account of Ella's ex-husband's new marriage, in some detail, no doubt. Witnesses recounted later that Ella's wine glass fell with a crash to the floor. Soon after, the party broke up, the men from Omaha left, and Ella went up the stairs to her room muttering, "I too am happy."

In her bed sound asleep was her lover, William Prinn. As she sat upon the bed, Ella, just 31 years old, took a .32 caliber revolver from her table and putting it to her head, pulled the trigger. As Prinn awoke from the blast of the shot, he saw horror and panicked. In an attempt to escape through the rear of house, he encountered the house maid and blurted out that Ella had killed herself.

Following a police investigation, Ella's death was ruled a suicide. William Prinn resigned his county clerk position a week later. The madams and girls of Market Street rolled out their carriages and provided a fine funeral procession to Riverside Cemetery where Ella Wellington was laid to rest.

While the sad life of Ella should end here, it did not. Another admirer and frequent customer, Fred Sturges, was evidently quite distraught over the death of Ella. Cemetery personnel soon kept an eye on the young man who stayed for hours every day at Ella's grave. A few weeks into this daily ritual, Sturges evidently fell asleep at Ella's grave. The caretaker discovered him the next day, dead. The coroner found a large dose of morphine in his system, an obvious suicide. A photograph of Ella along with a final note was found in his clutched hand. He was buried next to his beloved Ella according to his last wishes.

DURANGO'S HISTORIC *STRATER HOTEL* SAW its share of tragic events. No more so than the death of Stella Dempsey. Stella lived on the fourth floor where she plied her trade as a prostitute. Her lonely life ended in suicide in 1910. Stella was the sister of famed prize fighter Jack Dempsey. Following her death, Dempsey arrived in Durango in a black limousine. He picked out the casket and small granite tombstone which marks Stella's grave in Durango's Greenmount Cemetery. He paid cash for the casket and wrote a check for the tombstone to the local monument company.[9] Following the brief funeral services, Dempsey left town, leaving Stella's gravesite cold and alone.

And then there was Pearl DeVere, the beloved madam of Cripple Creek, whose end remains a mystery.

Pearl arrived in Cripple Creek from Denver in 1893. The Silver Panic had gripped the nation, causing financial ruin in Denver. Pearl arrived in the rich gold mining camp, amid swarms of prospectors who were reeling with joy over the hundreds of thousands of dollars Cripple Creek gold was bringing in.

A woman who has been described as beautiful, and strong in stature, it is a pity no photograph exists of Pearl DeVere. Pearl was one of those ladies the "good" women of Cripple Creek didn't mention. Children were forbidden to walk near Myers Avenue where Pearl ran her establishment, a parlor house for entertaining the men of Cripple Creek.

Some say Pearl led a very hard life. As the stories pass from generation to generation, it can be said she led a very colorful life. Reportedly, she at one time was known as "Mrs. Martin," and was quite wealthy. Whether this is true or Pearl perpetuated the myth, no one knows.

At the age of thirty-one, she had a head for business, and made a very lucrative living from the beginning. Her ladies were encouraged to wear fine clothing and were paid well enough to afford it. The common women of Cripple Creek shuddered at these women who dared to shop on Bennett Avenue, forcing Marshal Wilson to regulate the shopping hours of "the girls."

Pearl could be seen almost daily, riding her fancy single-seated phaeton, complete with red painted wheels, and led by a beautiful team of black horses. She would wear a different elegant dress habit everyday, her derby hat cocked to one side, as she smiled brightly at people who stared at her.

She was full of fun and had a kind heart. She generously gave to the charity causes in town monetarily, for she knew her presence wasn't welcomed at the various functions.

After the great fires of 1896, which were caused by one of the girls at the *Central Dance Hall*, Pearl lost no time in rebuilding her establishment on Myers Avenue. This time, no expense was spared. Her new "Old Homestead House" was built of brick (with a pink tint) and contained two bathrooms in the two-story house. Crystal electric chandeliers adorned the ceilings, hand-painted wall paper from France gleaned throughout, and the finest hardwood furniture graced every room. There was a telephone and even an intercom system! An Edison phonograph, the first in the mining camp, played sweet music for all to enjoy. The tongues wagged in Cripple Creek: electricity, new fangled gadgets, and two bathrooms, when decent family folk had outhouses and coal lamps!

Pearl's new establishment drew a rich clientele, where references were required of the guests. A single visit to the *Homestead* cost between fifty to one hundred dollars! Only the finest of food and drink were served, along with the beautiful girls.

Pearl's *Homestead* enjoyed the greatest fame and most prestigious clientele. Pearl became legendary, but it would all be short lived.

Pearl DeVere died on June 5, 1897 of an overdose of morphine. Some contend it was intended, others say it was accidental. The facts were reported in the *Cripple Creek Times* newspaper on June 10, 1897, five days after her sad death. The paper reported: ". . . the body was taken to the Fairley-Lampman rooms and Coroner Marlowe sent for." The coroner ruled that an accidental overdose of morphine, to induce sleep, had caused the death of Pearl DeVere.

The previous evening, Pearl had hosted a lavish party. Her many guests were wined and dined and offered the services of the boarders. Music played well into the early morning hours. Upon retiring, Pearl was restless and took a dose of the morphine to sleep. Still dressed in her exquisite Paris-made pink chiffon ball gown, complete with sequins and pearls, Pearl eventually fell to sleep.

Shortly after taking the drug, one of her girls checked on her. Finding Pearl breathing heavily and unable to wake her, local Doctor Hereford was summoned and did all he could, but the morphine had taken effect. Pearl DeVere died at the young age of thirty-six.

Pearl was not her real name, of course. Few madams used their real name. It is said her family thought she designed dresses for the wives of Cripple Creek's millionaires, rather than provocatively entertaining the millionaires themselves. According to local legend, Pearl's sister arrived from the East for the funeral. Seeing the corpse of her sister with dyed auburn hair at Fairley Brothers and Lampman's funeral parlor, the sister also learned the truth of Pearl's profession. She immediately left Cripple Creek, never to be seen again.

Many citizens of Cripple Creek were shocked when they learned of the sister's behavior. Pearl's generosity was known throughout the camp, yet often ignored during Pearl's life. With her death, the townsfolk had endeared the madam to the hearts of Cripple Creek. *The Cripple Creek Times* ran a banner headline: *Cripple Creek can bury its own dead!* An auction was spearheaded by Johnny Nolon, Cripple Creek businessman and owner of the popular *Johnny Nolon Saloon*. However, during the arrangements an anonymous envelope containing $1,000 in cash, postmarked from Denver and addressed to Fairley Brothers and Lampman Undertakers, arrived, paying all expenses and directed that Pearl be buried in the elegant ball gown. There was much speculation as to who sent the money and instructions, yet it has never been determined.

Pearl was buried with much pomp and circumstance on a cold, cloudy June day in 1897. The fire department band led the procession, playing the "Death March." A full parade of carriages followed the hearse carrying a lavender casket covered with red and white roses, to the cemetery on the hill. Those in attendance included the common folk of Cripple Creek, the influential businessmen in three piece suits, and miners, as well as the girls of the *Old Homestead.*

Years later following the death of Pearl, the *Old Homestead* underwent a renovation (now open to the public as a museum). During the renovation, a door was found in the basement rubble. It had been shipped from Denver and addressed to Isabelle Martin. Was the story true? Was Mrs. Martin really Pearl DeVere? The truth may never be known, yet Pearl's legend is very well-known...at least in Cripple Creek.

❧ Holidays were, by and large, gay events, full of music and merriment, food, drink, and entertainment. The girls along the line always looked forward to the holidays, with the exception of Christmas. That most holy of holidays was strictly for families, and so the girls sat alone and lonely.

One can almost imagine the red light district of town, normally bustling with activity. But on Christmas, with the cold weather, snowy, slushy, and muddy streets, the district would be deserted, depressingly cold and desolate. It is not hard at all to understand why suicides and accidental overdoses rose sharply during this time of year, especially on the row.

Lillie was a denizen of Denver's Market Street when she committed suicide on a dark lonely Christmas night. She left a hand-written note next to a lily. The note was a poem:

> *Mad from life's history,*
> *Glad to death's mystery,*
> *Swift to be hurled-*
> *Anywhere, anywhere,*
> *Out of this world.*

———————⚜———————

End Notes: Chapter Four

1   *Colorado Springs Gazette.*

2   Wommack, *From The Grave.*

3   *Silverton Standard*, December 6, 1902

4   Mayme Rogers later bought the infamous bordello.

5   Bird, *Bordellos of Blair Street.*

6   Both quotes from the *Silverton Standard.*

7   Smith, *Rocky Mountain Mining Camps.*

8   Denver County Court records and the *Rocky Mountain News*, July 28, 1894.

9   *Family Craft Memorial* owner Duane Fiorini showed me the framed check, which was never cashed.

FIVE

"Hell, she was just a whore." — Woodrow F. Call
From Larry McMurtry's *Lonesome Dove*

Victims
of Violence

I t's day all day in the daytime, And there is no night in Creede!
Cy Warman wrote these words describing Creede, and for a time, it fit.
Silver was discovered once again, and in unbelievable quantities, in Colorado's
Rocky Mountains in 1889. A narrow canyon in Colorado's high country yielded
silver by the ton, and so a town called Creede was
hastily constructed of wood slabs and tents. In less
than a year, more than 10,000 people crammed into
the small canyon, searching for a chance at riches.
Little did they know that Creede and all its wealth
would be short lived.

> Mattie Lemmon, a Denver
> denizen, poisoned a few
> of her customers.
> Convicted of murder, she
> went to Canon City state
> prison, where she died at
> the age of 25.

More than half of Creede's population were made
up of bunco artists, pick pockets, thieves, gamblers,
and mining sharks. One writer wrote that "Creede
was a community born in violence."[1]

Creede was indeed a wild, unsettled town. Saloons, dance halls, and ladies of
the evening were in such high demand, tents were thrown up as soon as the soiled
doves arrived. There was no time for suitable construction. Up and down Willow

Creek, the prostitutes were a welcome sight. Among Creede's ladies of the night, were Kilarny Kate, Slanting Annie, Timberline Rose Vastine, and the Norman Queen. Marie Contassot was in Creede, before her days in Denver were cut short by murder. Another future Denver madam, Lillis Lovell, was also in Creede during the mining boom, as well as Calamity Jane and Poker Alice. Mattie Silks, of Denver fame, made a tidy sum in the Creede area, at Jimtown, a small hamlet a mile or so downstream. Mattie had looked over the settlement of Creede. Considering all the tents seemed to be clinging to the sides of the canyon walls, she moved downstream to a more suitable spot, one that was level.

Creede Lilly was one of the first soiled doves in Creede. Very popular, her small log cabin on the upper edge of the mining camp, along the banks of Willow Creek, stayed busy nearly around the clock. When she died in 1892, Creede's underworld gambling establishment paid for her burial in the pauper section of the cemetery. How she died is unknown.

In every society there are those bent on criminal activity. During the early years following Colorado statehood, overall crime was minimal, yet high in particular areas. Most crimes were committed by men. Prostitution was the exception. Because of the nature of prostitution, crimes by and large were committed by women. Crime statistics reported by the newspapers, women's organizations, and the like tended to sway the public's opinion toward reform.

Another member of Silverton's demimonde was Blanche DeVille, a woman who had a penchant for stealing. The local papers were full of crime reports regarding her thefts. However, one incident reported in the *San Juan Herald* of September 18, 1884, seems a bit contrived by the outcome:

Blanche DeVille was indicted by the grand jury in stealing $50 from Jessie Carroll. She had been bound over in the sum of $200 by Justice Earl for the same offense and she left town. Deputy Sheriff Leroy went to Durango but could not find her. Her bondsman, not willing to lose $200, went after her and brought her back, and retained John G. Taylor to defend her. The case was set for trial in the morning of the twelfth, when District Attorney Rood stated to Judge Gerry that he would nolle the case of grand larceny, and the defendant would plead guilty to the other indictment of assault and battery upon Jessie Carroll. That he had examined the matter, and thought the fine of $20 and costs would be about right . . . Jessie Carroll was not pleased with this disposition of the matter, as she says she has proof positive of the stealing, and that Blanche did not assault her, and *that the grand jury did not indict Blanche for assault. She thinks 'law is a queer thing.'*

One might wonder why Blanche received the lesser judgment and fine. Yet, two weeks later, the *Silverton Democrat* reported an unfortunate accident had occurred:

Blanche DeVille, one of the Blair Street doves, was out riding with her lover Tuesday evening and met with quite a painful accident. In returning to town from Howardsville it seems that her saddle turned and she was thrown violently to the ground. Her left collar bone was broken in two places. The fractured member was set by Drs. Brown and Presby and she is said to be doing very well at present.

An accident? A plot of revenge? A botched attempt at murder? The answer is unknown, as Blanche DeVille recovered and left Silverton, never to be heard from again.

While crime did occur in the world of prostitution, the percentages were no higher than in other social areas such as gambling, bank fraud, or politics. In actuality, criminal activity among the prostitutes was twofold. Yes, there were women who committed crimes including murder. There were also crimes committed against many of our ladies of the tenderloin — many of which went unpunished. The crime of physical abuse against a prostitute, *if* there was a conviction in a court of law, was typically reduced to a misdemeanor and a small fine levied.

Minnie Johnson and Sallie Harris operated cribs on Leadville's seamy side. The two were habitual criminals according to the Leadville papers. One paper declared: "Marshal Phelps buckled his armor a notch tighter during the night and made a descent on the sanctuaries occupied by Minnie Johnson and Sallie Harris, two of the nefarious nymphs of Coon row, who are not only customers in police court, but who are as skillful in rolling customers as any of the noted operators of the east."

The media had a great time recounting the stealing escapades of the pair, so much so that several letters to the editor on the subject were submitted and published. Evidently, the two had inside help on several of their capers, as the following illustrates:

To the City Marshal,

Anonymous letters as a rule are not worthy of attention, but I beg of you to take notice of this one, as it is written in the interest of law and justice, and the writer has good reason for withholding his name. There has been a great deal of talk about Bessie (Minnie) Johnson and Black Sally stealing $160 the other night and the officers paying no attention to it. The money can be traced up even to this very late hour. One of the girls, Bessie Johnson bought a cloak either at the Golden Eagle or Palace, and there was a large quantity of goods brought to her place last night after dark. I believe, marshal, the robbery can be traced up if you interest yourself in the case.[2]

Police records indicate Minnie and Sallie were arrested numerous times. Each time fines were either assessed or the charges were dropped and the tenderloin girls went on their merry thieving way.

The red light districts attracted all sorts of people, and the criminal element was a constant threat. The soiled dove was aware of the clientele and took measures, as best she could. All too often, she was simply overpowered.

Scarface Liz was said to have once been the most beautiful soiled dove in all of Leadville. Liz became involved in yet another seemingly on-going fracas between the various members of the evening sisterhood and various customers. One particular incident resulted in great trauma and tragedy for Liz. During the ruckus, her attacker threw acid into her face, leaving her scarred forever.

Thus, she became known as Scarface Liz. Following a lengthy recovery, a shamed and destitute Liz left Leadville for the only work she felt she could acquire given her disfigured appearance, a crib in Cripple Creek, where she eventually died of alcohol poisoning.

Our ladies of the tenderloin had their vicious members as well. Ida Mae Jones, known as "Black Ide," was one of the worst. Black Ide operated a small bordello on Market Street in Denver. She had a reputation of drinking and violence. It was said she would swing a ball bat against anyone when she was on a drunken spree. In one incident, she took the ball bat to Jennie Thompson, striking her several times. On August 1, 1890, she followed Steve Zimmer down Market Street and stabbed him to death.

Black Ide was sent to the state penitentiary, serving eight years of a fifteen-year sentence. Released from prison, Black Ide returned to Denver's Market Street and her old ways. She was arrested for beating one Jessie Smith nearly to death. How this did not violate her prison parole is unclear. In any case, a few weeks later, she was arrested again for menace, having pulled a gun on one of her customers. He had accused her of stealing more than $200. The money was not recovered. In 1902, Black Ide was charged and convicted of larceny and returned to the state penitentiary for a ten-year term. Ida Mae Jones was the first female inmate at Canon City to be pregnant. Prison records report the birth of her child, but nothing further. Black Ida was released from prison in 1905, and disappeared.

Maggie Moss, another Denver prostitute, was only seventeen years old when she helped a lover commit armed robbery. She spent the majority of her life at the state penitentiary.

The criminal element on Denver's Market Street caused high anxiety in 1884. The customers of the crib area seemed to be disappearing in frightening numbers. Blanche Morgan and Ardell Smith ran a two-room crib in the 2200 block of Market Street. Detectives began a surveillance of the crib area after receiving tips from the underworld. Blanche and Ardell were eventually arrested for the murder of William Joos. The modus operandi of the girls was to mix morphine into the customer's drink and then to rob him. They went too far with Joos. Incredibly, Blanche Morgan was released and served no time, while Ardell Smith received one year in the county jail. Mattie Fisher played a role in the crime and also received jail time for her efforts.

And there was Nettie Clark, a black woman, who was shot and left to die in a Denver alley in 1896; she was not yet thirty years old. Her killer was never found.

Another Market Street duo, Belle Warden and Mattie Lemmon, were charged with first-degree murder following the death of a customer named John Fitzgerald. His body was found by detectives in Cherry Creek, near the Colfax Avenue bridge. Accomplices in the murder were the women's lovers, who told how the killing occurred at Belle's crib: the victim's throat was cut. Both Belle and Mattie were sentenced to ten years at the state penitentiary. Mattie Lemmon died in prison in 1887; she was twenty-five years old.

Georgetown's red light district, Brownell Street, had its fair share of crime. Mattie Estes was the famous madam in the district, along with Mollie Dean. Mollie's real name was Mary Ann Nephue. A miner by the name of Arden Shea visited Mollie often and soon fell in love with her. When Shea saw Mollie at a social occasion with another man, he shot her, and then put a bullet in his head.

Another Georgetown prostitute, Lizzie Greer, first worked long, hot hours in a factory in the East, with an employer who made lewd and constant sexual advances. She chose employment at one of the bordellos in Georgetown. Soon, Lizzie caught the fancy of a miner named Sam Wade, and the two began living together. However, another miner named Hayes, who had been customer of Lizzie's, became jealous.

Tension grew between Wade and Hayes. Threats were exchanged. One night, the threats turned to violence. In the end, Hayes was dead. The following day, as law officers surrounded Wade and Lizzie's home, Wade grabbed Lizzie. He put a gun to her head and threatened death if the officers didn't leave. The officers patiently reasoned with Wade when suddenly he released Lizzie and fled the scene. The officers fired and Wade fell dead.

Ironically, Wade was buried in the same freshly dug grave as his victim; Hayes.

As for Lizzie, she left Georgetown shortly after the murders. Years later, she was found dead in a coal shed near the *Windsor Hotel* in Denver.

It seems crime, even in the tenderloin area, was often left to interpretation. Annie Ryan was the daughter of Elizabeth Ryan, who ran a bordello on Denver's Market Street. Elizabeth's top madams were her three daughters. Annie shot Maurice Lyon, a former policeman and lover of many years. Annie was later cleared; the act was determined to be self-defense. Another act of self-defense would take a court of law to prove.

Frankie Dodge was a very popular prostitute in Leadville. Eventually, Frankie fell in love with one of her customers, Henry Williams and it appeared that he had similar feelings for her. Within a short time, the two were living together; however, Frankie's happiness was short-lived. Williams fancied himself a high-stake gambler, and before long, Frankie was paying off his debts.

Frankie began to notice things missing from their rooms above her bordello. Little things, at first. Then Williams would leave town on business trips. As the number of trips increased, Williams demanded money from Frankie. Suspicious, Frankie made a few trips herself, following Williams.

In Kansas City, Frankie discovered her lover with another. She was Lida King, a one time prostitute of Leadville. Devastated, Frankie went back to Leadville, and soon, Williams followed. Eventually, the two reconciled. It wasn't long before Frankie noticed things were missing again. When her expensive fur coat was gone and Williams had left for yet another trip, Frankie realized the deceit had started again, and this time she had had enough. She ended the affair and went home to her mother's house in Denver. A few months later, Williams showed up, promising to leave Lida and marry Frankie. Frankie relented and the two moved back to Leadville.

Frankie went back to business and did well, for she bought Williams a watch and chain for his birthday, paying more than $200 cash. When Williams pawned the gift, Frankie confronted him. Williams became violent and, cursing, shoved Frankie. Grabbing a razor, he threatened her life. Williams left Frankie once again. Frankie bought a gun. She carried it at all times, concealed in the bustle of her dress. When she heard Williams was back in town, she reluctantly went to meet him, at the Pioneer Bar on State Street. The conversation immediately turned into an argument, with Williams forcing Frankie out the back door of the bar. In the alley the arguing continued, until Williams pulled the razor. Williams shoved Frankie, with the razor's edge near her face. Frankie retrieved her gun from her bustle and fired. Williams turned to run and Frankie fired again.

In 1889, a Leadville court found her not guilty of murder. Frankie Dodge again left Leadville, this time for good.

As one might imagine, the Colorado courts were quite busy with crime involving the soiled doves. Their appearances in court as either the accused or the accuser tended to further the negative community reaction.

Denver's Ida Martin is a perfect example. It is not known if she was actually guilty of the many crimes of which she was accused, for the charges were always dropped. But time after time she appeared in the court and her name appeared in the papers.

Ironically, Telluride's Marshal Jim Clark, a fellow who disliked soiled doves and detested patrolling that city's tenderloin, was gunned down in Telluride's tenderloin district in 1895. Clark left the *Brunswick Saloon* at Spruce and Colorado Avenue, where he was shot by a gunman atop the *San Juan Saloon*. Clark managed to make it to the cribs across the street, pleading for help, which he received, but to no avail.

Women can be quite cruel to one another, even more so in fits of jealousy. The *San Juan Herald* gives a great example:

A serious altercation occurred at the Odeon Dance Hall on Tuesday evening last at 10 o'clock between two frail sirens of that place. The cause was said to be jealousy and resulted in one women inflicting a severe stab upon the other between the shoulders. The offending party was arrested and given bail, was held for trial yesterday morning, when a hearing took place before Justice York, and the offend-

Denver Public Library

Telluride's *Brunswick Saloon*, in the heart of the Tenderloin district, was the site of murder. Marshal Jim Clark was shot in front of the saloon, but managed to make it across the street to the soiled dove crib area, where he later died.

Creede was a wild and reckless town when the soiled doves came to call

Newspaper sketch of Marie Contassot, a soiled dove and victim of Denver's "Jack the Ripper" murders.

MARIE CONTASSOT.

Many soiled doves saw the inside of jail cell for a variety of charges.

Bell Birnard's parlor house was located at 1952 Market Street, in the very block where the "Jack the Ripper" murders occurred.

er pleaded guilty, was fined the sum of $25 and costs, with a caution from the court not to repeat a similar offense.

Pretty, petite Mollie May arrived in Leadville in 1879, following brief careers in such places as the Black Hills and Cheyenne. Leadville boasted a population of more than 30,000, just a year after the great silver strike.

The mining camp was a wild and lawless place in 1879, but Mollie, small in stature, proved she could hold her own. Mollie May was undoubtedly Leadville's most famous madam.

Mollie was one of the few prostitutes who actually used her given name, Melinda May Bryant, when she purchased her first house at 129 West Fifth Street. With a multitude of bordellos on Fifth Street, Mollie had the misfortune of moving in next door to Leadville's siren, Sallie Purple. Competition along the row of Fifth Street was high, and soon turned personal. Sallie nurtured a hatred for Mollie, as Mollie earned a reputation for an honest house and her clientele steadily increased, while Sallie's business decreased.

Sallie and Mollie became arch rivals. Tempers often flared and loud arguments became part of the daily routine. Then late one night, the two argued again. According to the local papers, a highly disputed point regarding the merits of Connaught and Tipperary as birth places led to open warfare between the two women. Insults turned into gunfire between the two bordellos, owned by Mollie and Sallie. With guns aimed through the windows, soon the girls of both houses, as well as the guests were involved in the fracas. After an hour or so, everything quieted down, possibly due to the arrival of the police. What few girls were not hauled off to the jail house went on with business, and by daylight everything seemed to be back to normal. Amazingly, there were no injuries.

Elizabeth Marshall is another example of female jealousy and revenge. Lizzie as she was affectionately known, was a popular prostitute in Buena Vista. She was doing so well in her business and was in the process of buying property to start her own bordello, when jealousy and resentment turned into violence. Belle Brown, another Buena Vista soiled dove resented Lizzy's new-found popularity. One Saturday night, Belle decided she would take care of her rival. She supplied her customers with free drinks, sweet talked them, and then asked them to do her a little favor. The men gladly went over to Lizzie's establishment and proceeded to break up the place. They did that easily enough, and more.

During the melee, Lizzie was hit in the left eye. The injury caused permanent blindness in the eye and loss of muscular control. She was forever known as "Cock-eyed Liz." The perpetrators of the act felt badly about what they had done, and the entire red light district came to her defense. Belle Brown left town.

The women of the underworld were victims of violence in many different forms. One of many examples comes from the headlines of the *Victor Record*:

Peter Derioche, one of the French macs residing in the tenderloin district of Victor, created a sensation in that section of the city yesterday by beating his lady love until she was a sight to behold. He put the finishing touches on his work by breaking an incandescent globe over her face. The officers are looking for him but he has decamped for greener fields and pastures new.

A similar incident occurred in Fairplay, with far different results. Under the headline, "License Revoked," the *Rocky Mountain News* reported the following on December 6, 1882:

Samuel Marsh was a proud prosperous saloon-keeper of Fairplay upon whom the sun shone with peculiarly bright effulgence. But the sun shines brightly for him no more. He had a trusting wife. She trusted that he could whip her, but Monday, when they had an argument on family matters, Marsh nervously drew a revolver to meet the raise of a broom with which Mrs. Marsh had armed herself. It caused Mrs. Marsh to lose confidence in her husband and she invited him to disarm and meet in equal contest of hand-to-hand. He reluctantly complied with her request and they waded in. The battle was by no means prolonged. Marsh failed ignominiously. The city council revoked his license on account of not being able to keep order in his house, as evidenced by the fact that he could not whip his wife. With that came an attachment which closed him out completely.

An equally disturbing incident occurred in Silverton:

The tracks of blood leading from the Hub Saloon along 13th Street were the subject of much comment on Monday morning, and from the quantity of blood spilled it really seemed as though some one had bled to death. Subsequent inquiry elicited the facts that Frank Cooper, the proprietor of the Hub, had been cut in the hand while in an act of defending himself from an enraged woman, who sprang at him with a clasp knife. Frank caught the knife, and as the blade was drawn through, it left an ugly gash in the palm of his hand. The difficulty had begun in the fashion when it is said that Frank refused to dance with the woman, Nell Castrell, and she then followed him to the saloon with the results stated. — The La Plata Miner, December 5, 1885.

Nell Castrell later bought *Mattie's Boarding House*, a bordello located at the southwest corner of Blair and 12th Streets, only to lose it in 1888 for non-payment. This is the only original building standing today, intact in its 1880's appearance on Silverton's Blair Street.

In Telluride, Fannie Nash was shot to death during a game of cards. Her murderer was never captured and apparently the search was not a top priority. Fannie was a black dance hall girl at an establishment on Pacific Avenue that catered to the black clientele. On the night of October 29, 1902, the dance hall was very crowded with customers and dance hall girls. One customer had been playing cards with a group that included saloon girls, in particular, Fannie Nash. He suggested a game of a different sort, explained the game, and everyone at the table agreed. The game went on for quite some time, with Fannie winning the majority of the time. As Fannie won another card hand, she reached for the money and the man grabbed her hands. Ed Washington, the proprietor, separated the two, moved them to a separate room, yet the quarreling continued. The two were on opposite sides of the room when the man pulled a gun, and with both hands, aimed and fired at Fannie.

The bullet grazed her left elbow and went through her breast. Fannie managed to stumble a few feet before falling. She was dead. Meanwhile, the man rushed through the crowd, out the door and was gone forever. A meager attempt by the authorities was launched to search the town. A few hours later, it was reported there was no sign of the man. Nothing further was reported of the "incident." According to *The Telluride Daily Journal*, Fannie Nash was approximately thirty years of age, and had arrived in Telluride only a week previously, reportedly from Cripple Creek.

And there is this example from a Denver newspaper:

A shudder of horror swept through the ranks of the scarlet women of the half-world when they learned of the mysterious crime. Market Street is superstitious. There is a belief that one such murder is bound to be followed by two others in rapid succession. Every woman in the quarter believes this as firmly as she believes death is inevitable. Convinced of this fact, the half-world is in a state of excitement bordering on panic that nothing will assuage . . . A hush fell on Market street. Women awakened from their sleep by the first alarm dressed partially and hastened to the scene of the crime. In the dim light from the street lamps they stood about in groups before the door of the house of death and talked in whispers of the tragedy. — The Denver Republican, July 6, 1903

The Denver newspapers only added to the fear that gripped the residents of Market Street, and all of Denver, which started with what the papers dubbed "Strangler's Row," in 1894.

That fall of 1894 brought a bloody and chilling episode in Denver's early history. Within three months, three women were strangled in their own cribs. Suddenly the headlines of the Denver newspapers screamed with sensationalism; "Jack The Ripper," the papers wrote, now stalked the streets of Denver. There were reasons to be concerned; all victims to date had been murdered on the "row," all had been strangled, and all had been found with a towel in their mouths. Moreover, with no sign of forced entry, a stranger in the form of a customer now became the invisible suspect. Fear gripped the city, while the madams and ladies of Market Street lived in terror. Denver's famous madam, Mattie Silks, owned a fancy parlor house just down the way from the latest murder. To protect her girls, Mattie had iron bars installed on all the windows. Another legendary madam, Laura Evans, was so shaken by the killings of "Jack the Ripper," that she left Denver for good. For a time, most of the finer parlor houses along the row shut down or limited their business hours. Only the one-room establishments, or cribs, remained open, and even these women were terrified.

In September, Lena Trapper was choked to death in her crib at 1911 Market Street, with a piece of her own skirt. She was found on her bed. Trapper's one-time lover, Richard Demady was arrested and later acquitted.

The next month, on October 28, 1894, Marie Contassot was found dead in her crib at 1925 Market Street. The evidence was nearly the same as the Trapper murder. Contassot had been strangled with a cord and was found dead on her bed in a similar fashion as Lena Trapper.

Marie and her sister, Eugenie, were brought to America from their native France, by one Charles Chaloup. Chaloup, as it turned out, was also French, as well as a Denver-based pimp with a less-than-good reputation. Marie and Eugenie now served the Market Street clientele under Chaloup's pimp ruling iron fist. He would soon fall under suspicion of murder by the Denver police department. However, the number one suspect remained Tony Saunders, the man who alerted police to the murder. It had happened in the wee morning hours of that day, when Saunders ran from his home in the 1900 block of Market Street, frantically blowing a whistle. Three officers near the location heard the whistle as a signal for help and rushed to the scene. Pushing through the sizable crowd that had formed, the police gained access to the private residence at 1925 Market Street.

In the bedroom just off the parlor, the officers' gazes found Marie's corpse. Marie Contassot, only twenty-three years old, had been choked to death, leaving her face grossly discolored, swollen, and her eyes bulging from their sockets. Her neck was badly bruised. A large piece of rope was found near the body. There were no signs of forced entry.

Police discovered that their number one suspect, Tony Saunders (Sanders) was indeed a Denver policeman, but also went by an alias, Antonio Santopietro. It seems Antonio Santopietro was well-known on Market Street as a pimp, but not as a cop. However, according to police reports, while under interrogation, he professed his love for Marie, and swore (in broken English and Italian) he had nothing to do with her murder. He stated they had been lovers for over seven months and that she had just moved in with him less than a week earlier. Eventually he was released for lack of evidence.

Two weeks later, Kiku Oyama was found strangled with a towel, dead on her bed at 1957 Market Street. Oyama, aged nineteen, had only arrived in the United States a year earlier. Denver had very few Japanese prostitutes, and the murder of one so beautiful and so young set the women of Market Street into terror.

❧ FOLLOWING THIS THIRD HORRIFIC EVENT, the murders stopped and no one was ever caught, tried, or convicted.

> The dizzy females of the city, who toil not, are making it lively for the policemen of late. Whenever they have to pull in one of the frail creatures, they find that they have war on their hands, and it takes from two to five to land the law-breaking female in the cooler.[3]

One of Leadville's notorious prostitutes was Kate Armstead, a black lady who had a small bordello at 137 West State Street. It is said she was a mean, vicious woman, hated by many on the row. In any case, a story is told of her total lack of compassion, when she literally threw a drunken, diseased member of her house, who could no longer perform her "household duties," out into the street. The girl was left there, where she died. Another tale of Kate's unsavory demeanor, was when she threw out another girl, dying of disease. When Kate learned the girls had gone to another house for refuge, she waited until she saw the girl outside the house, and threw lye on her.

On the morning of July, 7, 1881, Kate was found in her cabin near death. She had been sliced wide open with a knife, from her lower neck to her breast, as well as gashes on her arms and stomach. Andrew Lewis, a mulatto, was later arrested for the crime.

Yet, this brush with death did not cure Kate's wicked ways. She sold her house to a William Jones, who owned the saloon next door to Kate's, and Kate left town. Evidently things didn't work out for Kate, as she was back in Leadville a few months later.

In an effort to regain her house, she told the authorities Jones had defaulted on the sale. Jones, the police, and the courts disagreed with Kate. She swore she would burn down the place, and perhaps she did. Very near midnight a few days later, William Jones thought he smelled coal oil. Rising from his bed, he checked the situation. To his horror, he found the Armstead house on fire. The fire destroyed the house and Jones' saloon, as well as a few other establishments.

Kate Armstead had evidently left Leadville on the late train, as she was never found by the investigating police.

Laura Evans, the beloved madam of Denver and Salida, recounted a horrible incident to researcher Fred Mazzulla.[4] During her early prostitute days in Leadville, Mayor Samuel Nicholson was a frequent customer. One evening, it seems the good mayor began biting Laura, taking a "piece out of my thigh the size of a quarter. I had to go to Dr. Law to have it cauterized." A few days later, she and a friend were arrested on the streets of Leadville, following a horse racing accident. As the patrolman was escorting the women to jail, the mayor came upon the scene, and noticing Laura, asked of the officer what the problem was. Laura tenderly reached toward her thigh and said, "I think I've hurt myself." The stunned officer stared at Laura for an explanation, but none came. The mayor convinced the officer to release the girls, which was done, and "His Honorable Holiness," as Laura termed the mayor, left the scene with much haste. According to Laura, the mayor never called on her again.[5]

Violence toward the soiled doves of Cripple Creek became so bad that the ladies of the tenderloin organized the *Dance Hall Girls Protection Association*, which in effect became a statement and little else. Prostitutes were victims of crimes in many ways, and not always violent in nature. The following is one example.

Laura Winnie, proprietress of a pretentious Fifth Street mansion in Leadville, fell to the charms of a dapper banker by the name of Frank De Walt.[6] Apparently, the two had a very romantic relationship, with De Walt on one occasion presenting Laura with a stunning nine diamond cross necklace.

The romance came to an end in the summer of 1884, shortly after the First National Bank of Leadville closed its doors. The city officials had been investigating De Walt, president of the bank, on suspicion of bank fraud. Gathering evidence and testimony, they turned the case over to the government, by state and federal law, for prosecution. Charged with bank fraud, De Walt went to trial in federal court in Denver. It is said Laura paid for her lover's defense counsel. But in the end, after much testimony detailing crooked deals, false accounting, forged documents, and out-right theft, De Walt was found guilty and sentenced to ten years of hard labor in the U.S. penitentiary at Laramie, Wyoming.

Laura Winnie's story then takes a strange twist. Laura leased out her Leadville bordello and moved to Montrose, where she opened a house of pleasure. Laura had a few girls working for her and business was going fairly well, although not as well as it had been in Leadville. Range riders and trail bosses were the majority of Laura's clientele.

Not long after Laura established herself in her new house in Montrose, she met an eloquent stranger, new to town. The gentleman wore the finest of western apparel and carried himself with an air of confidence, along with his unique cane. Yet, a bit of mystery seemed to surround him. In any case, Laura became infatuated with him and seemingly, he with her. Laura was at a happy time in her life.

Meanwhile, a local detective had also taken an interest in the new stranger. Quietly, he watched, observed and took note of details. When Laura walked into his office one morning, the detective was a bit taken aback, but not totally surprised as Laura explained the reason for her visit. She was very upset about a treasured necklace given to her by a dear friend some years ago. She had awakened that morning to find the cross necklace on the floor, minus the nine diamonds it had once held. The kind detective asked questions of the distraught Laura and after the very personal interview, Laura said she could not believe "Mr. Thompson," her special friend, could have anything to do with this. But the detective did believe exactly that. Apparently, Thompson had left town for Denver the previous evening on business, but promised to return to Laura.

The detective immediately went to work investigating Thompson's background. The local banks and cattlemen did not know the man; he had no business dealings in the area. The detective took the next train to Denver.

As luck would have it, as the detective entered a saloon at a stopover in Salida, he spotted his man. Thompson had been drinking for quite awhile, and as the detective engaged him in conversation and more drinks, Thompson presently laid his cane on the bar. Picking up the cane, the detective noticed the lop-sided end and heard a faint rattle. Immediately leaving the bar, the detective found a hotel room and struggled with the cane. Presently, the end unlocked, spilling the contents into the detective's palm.

Returning to the bar with the cane, the now very inebriated Thompson reached for his cane, asking how the detective came to have it. The detective said he had stolen it from Thompson and inquired as to the whereabouts of the diamonds. Dumb-founded, Thompson tried to regain his composure. When he failed to reply, the detective retrieved the cane and alerted the police.

Laura's precious diamonds were returned to her, along with a broken heart, for Thompson never returned.

LaVerne recalled several incidences of violence and how her employer, Miss Laura Evans, handled the occurrences:

We girls never locked the doors to our rooms. We kept them unlocked, so in case the man started getting too rough with us — biting us, twisting our breasts too hard, clawing us with his fingernails right down there where it hurt us the most, well, a girl who was starting to get that treatment would yell for help. Someone would be sure to come to help-and maybe quite a few would come to help. We had no man bouncer at Miss Laura's. But what chance would the customer have if, say for instance, eight other girls came running into the room to protect her? If a man tried to hurt me, I'd knock his head off-or try to. I've had to slap the hell out of a lot of them — that's how some of them got their satisfaction, though. You run across all kinds in this business . . . you just close your mind to it.[7]

One only has to dig through a few old newspapers, county court records, or cemetery histories to realize the "happily ever after" scenario was rare in the world of prostitution. Alcoholism, drug abuse, and murder were more likely to be the end of many soiled doves.

Mabel Brown was only twenty years old when she was brutally murdered in her crib at 1931 Market Street in Denver. A week earlier Antoine Kenhan, a street peddler, had been found murdered in a similar fashion. And again, panic gripped Market Street. The front page of the *Denver Times* dated July 6, 1903 read:

Horrible Deed of a Strangler: Mabel Brown Bound and Choked to Death in a Market Street Resort. This morning at an early hour the dead body of Mabel Brown . . . was found in a bedroom in her house, 1931 Market Street. She had been strangled to death.

Young Mabel was raised in North Denver by her father, following her mother's death. "Big Swede" Brown, as her father was known, was a well-known saloon keeper in lower downtown. Mabel attended school in North Denver and Sunday school at Highland Park Presbyterian Church, and later found domestic work. Within a short period of time, Mabel was found living in a crib on Denver's "Row," where she fell in with the likes of Harry Challis, a hot-headed local bar tender, as well as a surly wine dealer named Samuel Holzweig.

On the night of the murder, July 5, 1903, Challis left work on a break, to inform Mabel he would be working late and to meet him at a later time, as they met every night. Unable to arouse her by a knock at the door, he opened the door, which to his surprise was unlocked. There, he said he found Mabel lying on the bed, dead with a cloth in her mouth. Eventually alerting the police, Challis became the prime suspect.

Police reports, described in detail in all the newspapers, stated the crime scene was undisturbed. On the bed near Mabel's hand were two dollar coins, the bed clothes were ruffled, as if to suggest a struggle by Mabel. No furnishings were disturbed and nothing seemed to be missing. The police felt this was not a robbery gone bad. However, handwritten letters by Mabel were found on the floor, torn in small pieces. One piece mentioned owing two dollars. Was Mabel waiting unknowingly for her killer?

Challis became the number one suspect, along with Holzweig, a one time lover of Mabel's. According to reports, Mabel had broken off with Holzweig several months prior to her death, after taking up with Challis. The two men had a confrontation resulting in a bar room brawl. Holzweig left town after that, only to return shortly before Mabel's murder. Although he was seen in another parlor house on Market Street on the night of the murder, he became a suspect when it was learned he had threatened her life when she left him.

Whoever committed the murder of Mabel Brown was deliberate in the act. She had been strangled, her hands tied to the bed. The autopsy revealed water in the lungs, possibly to revive her, or probably to ensure death, will never be known.

The murder was never solved.

A local miner for one of the mines near Telluride visited a pretty young soiled dove on Pacific Avenue once too often. Jess Munn had a fondness for the girl, and, by all account, the girl liked him. The local marshal, Art Gigline, also had an eye for the lady, and became a regular customer. When Munn found out, he threatened the marshal. The marshal took Munn's gun and left the premise, escorting the young prostitute. Enraged, Munn procured another gun and set out for Marshal Gigline. He found his man in the street, yelled at him and four shots rang out. The marshal was dead and the miner was on the run. Munn was later captured, convicted and sent to the state penitentiary, where he was later killed in an escape attempt. As for the girl, her identity and what became of her are lost to history.

Liverlip was a prostitute in Leadville, where she was fairly popular. Where or what her name derived from, is not known, perhaps it became her new name after her face was carved up. In any case, Liverlip encountered a customer who was not happy with her services. In a rage, the customer took a razor to her face, disfiguring her forever. Horrified and humiliated, Liverlip left Leadville. She found work in the crib area of Cripple Creek's Poverty Gulch, where she encountered another unhappy customer. The man took some sort of sharp object to her face and body, leaving her barely alive.

Yet, Liverlip lived, recovered and regained her strength, and her life. She stayed in Cripple Creek, but changed her occupation to that of a bootlegger. It is said she did a great business with many, if not all, of the Myers Avenue establishments, who became her best customers.

Effie Moore was a seventeen year old dancer at the *Palace Theatre* on Denver's Blake Street. One evening as she mingled with customers, as required, she met a good looking, charming gambler. His name was Charles E. Henry, who was only nineteen years old. Evidently, a whirlwind courtship ensued and the two planned marriage. Rumors abounded at the Palace, as is typical in such atmospheres, and soon young Charlie was seeing red with jealousy fueled by alcohol.

According to police records, a drunken Charles Henry entered a private box at the Palace Theatre on the night of November 13, 1887. During the variety performance on stage, pandemonium broke out. As four gun shots rumbled from the box above the stage. Below, Effie Moore lay dead in a pool of blood. Henry was immediately arrested and as the funeral date approached, he offered to pay all expenses, as did Ed Chase, owner of the Palace Theatre. Charles Henry was later acquitted of all charges.

Lake City is where Jessie Landers plied her trade. Clara Ogden, the glamorous madam, owned the two-story bordello, where a grand party was in full swing on the night of June 11, 1896. Suddenly the music stopped, and the dancing ceased, as gunfire rang out. For a moment it seemed as if everyone froze in time. Then a few of the girls began to scream. A dead man lay on the ballroom floor. Another shot rang out: this one came from outside the bordello. Jessie Landers lay in the dirt, bleeding. When it was all sorted out, it seems a terrible mistake had turned deadly.

Young Jessie Landers was about to leave the sporting life forever. She had become engaged to twenty-year-old Louis Estep. Estep was considered to be a fine, upright member of the community. On that fateful night, Estep attended the party. Also in attendance was Frank McDonald, a known pimp. When Jessie saw the two men together in conversation, something in Jessie snapped. She grabbed her gun and fired in the direction of the two men. Jessie immediately realized what she had done as her betrothed, Louis Estep, lay mortally wounded. Jessie ran out the door and shot herself. Her wound wasn't fatal, but Estep died of complications and Jessie was tried for murder.

Clara Ogden circulated a petition in the community, requesting the minimum sentence for Jessie. Before the judge passed his sentence, he reminded the court of the nature of the crime and such tragedies being a direct result of the prostitution lifestyle. Jessie Landers was then sentenced to five years in the state penitentiary for voluntary manslaughter. She never revealed why she killed her betrothed.

Within two years of the shooting and sentencing of Jessie Landers, Lake City's tenderloin district faded into the past. A city ordinance said in part:

Any person who shall keep a bawdy house, (house of ill fame) . . . house for promiscuous dancing . . . within the limits of the town of Lake City, or within three miles . . . thereof . . . to suffer a subject fine of not less than five dollars nor more than one hundred dollars for each offense.

Madam Clara Ogden closed the doors of the *Crystal Palace* for good and left Lake City for parts unknown.

She was not alone, as madams across the state systematically boarded windows, turned out the lights, and locked the doors in search of safer locales.

In May of 1900, a young frail woman arrived in Lake City. Mysterious at first, once the identity of the woman became known, citizens in Lake City remembered an event they had hoped to forget.

Jessie Landers, the prostitute, convicted of manslaughter for the death of her betrothed, Louis Estep, had been released from the state penitentiary, after serving four years. Jessie had returned to Lake City and the home of a friend. Long suffering from tuberculosis, she died on the morning of May 16, 1900. Jessie was buried in an unmarked grave at the city cemetery. Some say her grave was near that of Louis Estep. The *Lake City Times* obituary gave a fitting eulogy:

. . . prejudices are hard to overcome, and kind hearts and tender hands did not interest themselves in this sad case until it was too late. May the change called death be an awakening to a brighter life, with no horrible dreams such as beset her temporal career.

End Notes: Chapter Five

1   Jessen, *Colorado Gunsmoke.*
2   Griswold and Griswold, *History of Leadville and Lake County.*
3   *The Leadville Evening Chronicle,* February 3, 1883.
4   Mazzulla Collection, Colorado Historical Society.
5   Miller and Mazzulla, *Holladay Street.*
6   *Carbonate Chronicle,* August 29, 1885.
7   Mazulla Collection, Colorado Historical Society.

SIX

Having seen much of life, my heart often warms with sympathy for the fallen.
— Reverend George M. Darley -1876

Angels of Mercy

A nnie Rooney, a beloved soiled dove of Cripple Creek's Myers Avenue, was found near death. The local newspaper reported:

. . . she endeavored last night to end the ills she knows so well by taking carbolic acid. Dr. Wright was summoned and, after an hour's hard work, restored the woman to consciousness. Will she live to reform and thank the doctor, or has he only rescued her for a plunge into greater depths?"

The *Boulder County Herald* reported:

Lou Bunch, Central City's famed madam was known for her kindness, contributing to charities, and often helping in a health crisis.

One of the demimonde, evidently tired of life, took a dose of laudanum and came near dying. She is 19 years old and goes by the name of Mamie Myers. She attempted suicide last Wednesday, but Dr. King came to the rescue. Last night her female companions worked over her all night and saved her.

Both women in these stories lived. While their ultimate fate is unknown, with the help of doctors and their fellow soiled doves, they were brought through their

ordeals. Our ladies of the tenderloin, with their caring hearts, brought many through equally trying times in our state's history.

As men were allured by prostitutes, so prostitutes were allured by charity. Although the business of prostitution provided services sexual in nature, it did not, contrary to definition, cause a lack of character.

The soiled doves indeed contributed much to Colorado's frontier towns. With their female charm came a sense of refinement, however limited it may have been. Many actually took part in the development of the town, albeit behind the scenes. They grubstaked miners, did their laundry and mending, and volunteered during a crisis or medical emergency. Many mountain mining camps experienced untold deaths due to epidemics that so often plagued these areas. In fact, the prostitutes were always, without exception, the first to volunteer their services. They nursed the sick men, cooked and cleaned, spoon fed the victims, and helped bury the dead.

Legends are born out of such tragic circumstances, and many a Colorado mining town had a *fair angel* story.

In Durango, a woman known only as Betty, a popular madam, was also a very charitable person, known to give freely to many churches and town emergencies. Bessie Rivers, Durango's beloved madam, was equally well-known for her many acts of charity. Bessie championed many causes, soliciting donations from the other bordellos for charitable purposes.

Established in 1880, Durango was a product of the Denver and Rio Grande Railroad. Almost overnight, the population of the new town swelled dramatically. No mountain town before or since grew so fast and unexpectedly due to the railroad. The railroad brought businessmen, investors, bankers, miners, farmers, ranchers, and . . . women. Durango prospered and businesses flourished. The town did so well, in fact, that there were two red light districts. The "line" stretched along Railroad Avenue, today's Narrow Gauge Avenue. The second tenderloin area was on the west side of Main Street. Some of the better-known houses of ill-repute were the *Clipper Dance Hall*, the *Silver Bell Dance Hall*, and the *Cutter Club*.

Disaster struck Durango in the summer of 1889. Fire exploded near the downtown area and quickly spread north, and on the east side of Main Street. While the tenderloin district was spared, much of downtown, including all three of the town's churches were destroyed. Durango citizens quickly pulled together in their time of crisis. Soon the town was in the midst of rebuilding, this time with brick. As the brick buildings went up on the east side of Main Street, the madams on the west side of the street took notice. Backed with their own money in some cases, and by — shall we say — business investments, for business was very good in Durango, the "Main Street Madams" began to rebuild *their* side of the street. With new buildings came new furnishings and the madams spared no expense. From the ceiling to the floor everything glittered, with soft light and fine furniture. Even the beds and the mattresses were replaced with the finest pieces available. It must have been quite a time in Durango.

OUR LADIES OF THE TENDERLOIN often supplied much more than sexual pleasure. By virtue of their womanhood, the soiled dove, more often than not, was a kind-hearted soul. It was not unusual, therefore, that a fallen girl might sew buttons, mend clothing, or darn socks for a lonely miner in need. At the onset of sickness, it was always the soiled dove who was first to provide care.

Blanche Burton, thought to be the first madam of Cripple Creek, later retired to Colorado City. She was known and respected in that community for her charitable donations and volunteer work for the poor. In fact, just the day before she died in a tragic fire in 1909, Blanche spent the last of her money for the month on a ton of coal, much of which she gave away, a regular monthly ritual for Blanche. This would be her final act of charity.

During the Spanish Influenza epidemic of 1918, Fanny Wright, known as "Jew Fanny," offered her services as a nurse at Silverton's pest house. The building, located a mile north of town, was used strictly for the diseased, who were held in quarantine. Sick miners, townsfolk, and children were all taken to the pest house during the flu epidemic. It is said that the local death rate was low, due in part to Fanny's hard work and dedication.

During the economic panic of 1873, Jennie Rogers supported her girls when there was little or no business and took in many others until they could return to their families.

During the Denver mob riots against the Chinese in 1880, Market Street madam Lizzie Preston opened her bordello to aid the Chinese. When a group of mobsters gathered at her door, Lizzie stepped out to the porch with a shotgun. She held the group at bay, backed by a dozen of her girls armed with stove pokers, champagne bottles and high heeled shoes! It must have been quite a sight when deputy sheriff Roberts and his men finally arrived on the scene. Before the riots ended, Lizzie gave shelter to more than thirty Chinese.

⚘ Colorado legend says Silver Heels was a dance hall beauty in the South Park area.¹ Many accounts or versions of the fabled story exist, but most center the story at either Fairplay or the nearby mining camps of Alma or Buckskin Joe. The story goes that the fair-haired beauty stepped from the stagecoach and astonished the miners with her beauty. She worked as a dance hall girl and gave sexual favors, and the miners loved her. She received her name from the miners who were so enchanted by her and, her unique silver-colored slippers.

According to the legend, a smallpox epidemic hit the mining camp of Buckskin Joe in 1861, and that the beautiful harlot was one of the very few not stricken with the sickness. She nursed the sick back to health, cared for the dying and comforted the bereaved. It is said that eventually Silver Heels (for no one is sure of her real name) became stricken with the disease and disappeared from the camp.

The recovered miners, in an effort to repay Silver Heels for her acts of kindness, collected donations and set out to find her, but to no avail. It is said the miners chose to name the mountain nearest Buckskin Joe, Mount Silver Heels in her honor.

Years later, as the legend has it, a woman, heavily veiled and dressed in black, was seen on several occasions at the cemetery, weeping softly. They said it was Silver Heels, her beauty scarred by the smallpox she had secretly suffered, her heart scarred by the tragedy of so many deaths. Silver Heels, the soiled dove, now became the angel of mercy.

A wonderful story of heroism during a tragedy, makes a great Colorado legend. Yet, it is just that: a legend.

There is no record of a smallpox epidemic in Alma, Buckskin Joe, Fairplay or any of the other nearby towns. In fact, Park County medical records reveal no sickness of epic proportions in the years from 1860 to 1864, the existence of the "boom gone bust" mining era of Buckskin Joe, as well as Alma and Fairplay.² Perusing the archives of the *Fairplay Flume*, which did not exist prior to 1879, it is revealing to note a column in each edition entitled "20 Years Ago." Throughout the paper's first year (1879,) there is no a mention of a smallpox epidemic "20 Years Ago."³ The two papers in existence at the time in Buckskin Joe (1860) both folded with no records available. Walking through the cemeteries of the area, one discovers only a few graves in each cemetery with the dates of 1863, even allowing for space for unmarked graves. More important, both the Fairplay cemetery and the cemetery at Buckskin Joe were created in 1863, a full two years after the supposed epidemic. Yes, cemeteries did exist on private lands; however, in cases of epidemics, any given town or mining camp without a cemetery previously, incorporated land for a cemetery immediately, both for sanitary and bereavement considerations. This was not done in any of the three towns mentioned in the legend of Silver Heels.

Mount Silver Heels is listed on Colorado maps only as early as 1866, and officially by the Hayden Survey in 1873, adding even more curiosity to the story.

The Silver Heels of Buckskin Joe isn't the only "soiled dove with a heart of gold" legend in Colorado. According to records of the Hinsdale County Historical Society, when a dance hall girl by the name of Maggie Hartman died, the local paper had this comment:

> . . . the Silverheels of Lake City, died after nursing an ailing miner. Reverend Darley read the burial services . . . shaking hands and speaking a kind word with each of the dance hall girls who attended the service.

𝒬 COLORADO SUFFERED MANY CASUALTIES DURING the Spanish Influenza epidemic of 1918. Salida was no exception. Short of nurses, it was Salida's madam, Miss Laura Evans, who went to the doctors and health officials at the hospital.

> Tell you what I'll do. I'll shut down the house and the cribs. You put my girls in nurse uniforms and I'll send them around town to help. They aren't trained nurses, but you can use the help. Keep it secret.

Following the flu crisis, one of Laura's girls known as Jesse was asked by a grateful couple to stay on as housekeeper. She expressed her thanks and said she would go back to Miss Laura. Laura's girls were indeed loyal.[4]

Pearl Eastman was another soiled dove who helped to heal the sick during the flu epidemic. Pearl worked in one of the cribs on Silverton's Blair Street, where she had an on-again, off-again relationship with a local cook named of George Sitter. The two had a terrible quarrel and eventually mended the relationship when the flu epidemic hit the town. Pearl worked tirelessly at nursing the sick and caring for the families who lost loved ones. Soon Pearl became ill. George tried to save her as death slowly took over. She was buried in one of the many unmarked graves that claimed several during the epidemic.

Henrietta Denoyer, (left) as a young hair dresser outside the shop Miss Laura Evans and her girls had their hair done.

What could be thoughts in the mind of this lovely soiled dove? Hope and dreams, or sadness and despair? If only her gaze on a beautiful flower could tell us...perhaps it does.

Louisa Bunch, a popular madam known as Lou to everyone in Central City, ran her bordello on Pine Street. Lou was as a kind, caring woman, often giving to charity. Lou and her girls were known to offer help to their fellow citizens on several occasions in times of sickness and sorrow. The folks of Central City came to view Lou as a beloved citizen, despite her profession.

At the age of twenty-one, Laura Bell McDaniel left her native Missouri for Colorado, eventually settling in Colorado City a few years later, where she opened her business of pleasure one block south of Colorado Avenue. The *Tribly House*, as it was known, became so popular for the politicos, that tunnels were actually built under Colorado Avenue, connecting to the red light district, including a direct tunnel to Laura Bell's place, in an effort to elude the public. However, the favoritism of politicians toward Laura Bell was short-lived. By 1917, the Conformist Movement succeeded in closing down the red light district, and Laura retired to pursue more conventional activities. Laura turned her attention to those less fortunate, providing shelter, raising money, and even personally lending a hand to the needy.

On a January day in 1918, Laura Bell, accompanied by her namesake niece, was driving a blind miner to Denver for a medical appointment, when Laura's 1910 Mitchell sedan was in a serious accident. Laura's niece died at the scene, while Laura, severely injured, died the next day of internal injuries. Amazingly, the blind miner survived with few injuries.

The story of Queenie is both touching and tragic. Queenie was a part-time dance hall girl in Cripple Creek during that city's booming years around the turn of the century. Queenie was described as tall, thin and with straight black hair. Queenie was also a nurse who worked part time caring for sick people in their homes, and often did the cooking and cleaning for her patients with no additional charges. Queenie was nearly always available when sickness broke out, and so, was held in high regard in Cripple Creek — with the exception of her live-in lover. Evidently he was a miner who had been hurt sometime back, and couldn't or wouldn't get a job. He relied on Queenie's income and it was never enough. By all accounts, he was a mean, vicious man. Why Queenie stayed with him until her death will never be known.

Jim Ridell related the story of Queenie in several interviews with Fred Mazzulla.[5]

As a young teenager, Ridell said he got to know both Queenie and her lover when he delivered groceries to their tiny cabin outside of town. According to

Ridell, who knew of the constant fights and abuse, Queenie had told him during a delivery that his services would no longer be needed. She said her boyfriend had accused her of something awful, and closed the door.

The next day Queenie's body was found — she had committed suicide. As Cripple Creek prepared for her burial, rumors rolled through town. Where was the boyfriend? Was it true? Did Queenie burn him (give him venereal disease)?[16]

Queenie's funeral was a fine affair. Most businesses were closed and nearly the entire town walked to the small hillside cemetery to pay their respects to the woman who had so often cared for their sick loved ones. However, Queenie's man did not attend the funeral.

Following the funeral, a group of men gathered. Talk soon turned to Queenie and the absence of the boyfriend at the funeral. Then the undertaker offered an observation on the matter. He said Queenie couldn't have burned the man. He said he knew because he prepared her body for the burial. Again, Ridell supplied historians of his account of that day, a day he said he would never forget as long as he lived.

After the declaration from the undertaker, the group was now an angered mob, demanding where to find the low down so and so. Young Jim Ridell told the group where the cabin was. It was much later in the night, when Jim learned someone had hanged Queenie's man.

The *Denver Evening Post* of February 20, 1897, carried an intriguing article related to a bordello in Florissant. The article said in part that the soiled doves, "God's own girls," were rescuing birds who were hurt by flying into the newly constructed telephone wires, and caring for them until they were well enough to fly away again.

During the Great Depression of the 1930s, the soiled doves of Colorado often gave out food. Although it was by the back door, the food was given generously to many hungry families. Newspaper accounts across the state, during this harsh time in American history, are full of good deeds, great and small, including generous acts by prostitutes. In Silverton, Frances Belmont, a popular, kind woman of the line, donated food to the churches for the needy. She also volunteered her time to shelters to care for the poor during the Depression years. She continued to operate her bordello (at reduced pricing) until her death, caused by cancer, in 1936.

Henrietta Denoyer of San Diego, California, now in her eighties, recalled many Depression era stories in interviews with the author. Henrietta was a teenager in Salida during that time and worked as a hairdresser at the Blue Moon Beauty

Shop, where many of her customers were the ladies of Miss Laura Evans' bordello. Although Henrietta never met Laura, she occasionally saw her "big black car" on the streets of Salida. Henrietta's future husband, Lawrence, was a sixteen year old gas station attendee who often pumped the gas for Laura. Henrietta recalled many stories she heard of Laura and her girls offering charity and that many times the girls would give leftover bread and biscuits to the men who would knock at the kitchen door. Henrietta said Laura's girls were often the first to help in town emergencies and were also great tippers when she fixed their hair!

Creede's angels of mercy came silently to the aid of a Mrs. Majors, when her house caught on fire and was dangerously close to burning down. Mrs. Majors was frantically moving what valuables she could out of the house:

Then came a never to be forgotten surprise. The street door swung open and three women of the demimonde came up the stairway! The one who first reached the top addressed me by name, and said it would be impossible to save our building, and that they had come to help me, to forget who they were and tell them what to do. When told the things in the hall were ready to be taken, they carried them out, even the heavy trunks, then stood guard over them. The street was filled with swearing men and weeping women, some with babes in their arms, little children carrying favorite toys and dolls. But the fire was finally under control. Then these women carried our belongings back. I felt most grateful to those poor out casts, and would gladly have treated them with kindness, but they never spoke to me again. They gave me no chance to speak to them.[7]

The tenderloin district of Telluride included the *Brunswick Saloon* and *The Senate*, while the cribs were located primarily on Pacific Street. Along Telluride's Pacific Avenue, the seamy side of town, night life sprawled along both sides of the street. Saloons and bordellos were the combination in Telluride, as in many cramped mountain mining towns. Saloons were on the main floor, while the girls worked upstairs in such places as the *Pick and Gad*, *Big Swede*, and the *Idle Hour*. The cribs were at the end of the street, where a few still remain today, as does *The Senate* and *Pick and Gad*.

At *The Senate*, one of the more popular madams was "Big Billy," the same "Big Billy" from Silverton. While in Telluride, Billy was known to lend a helping hand with the needy and the sick. It is even said the society women of the "north side" of town held Billy in high esteem, although somewhat guarded.[8] Billy evidently showed a different side of her nature after leaving Silverton! The Senate also employed a young Jack Dempsey as dishwasher for a time.

Ellen Smith, a Leadville prostitute, wrote a long letter to a friend of hers, Mattie Finch. Mattie had been struggling for quite awhile, probably due to her alcoholic problems. Ellen, who was doing a fair business with several cribs she owned, offered Mattie a crib and a chance to get on her feet. Mattie arrived in Leadville in the summer of 1887 and, promising Ellen her drinking days were over, set up her own crib for business.

Unfortunately, not even a week later, Mattie went on a drinking spree. At the end of the second week, Ellen had no choice. She could not reason with Mattie or talk any sense into the woman who was constantly in an intoxicated state and foul mouthed. Ellen reluctantly threw her out.

A few days later, Mattie appeared on the streets and alleys along the tenderloin. Her appearance was filthy, her manner was deplorable. She begged for whiskey and if she received some; she loudly cursed for more. As sad as the situation was, it was about to get worse.

On the morning of August 15, 1887, Mattie was again roaming the streets begging for whiskey. By noon, a drunken Mattie fell into the street gutter. A good Samaritan carried her off the discarded shanty she had been living in. Around sunset, a pathetic Mattie was again roaming the streets. Late into the night, she made her way to the crib of a fellow denizen and begged to be let in.

It is said Mattie begged for milk and within the hour, she was dead. Several girls of the tenderloin gathered at the crib. Soon Ellen arrived, pushing her way through the crowd, which now included policemen. She knelt beside the corpse of her sad old friend. Ellen took Mattie's hands into her own, and sat silently for the longest time. Moonlight glimmered throughout the cracks of the wooden structure, highlighting the tears on Ellen's ebony cheeks.

Presently, Ellen folded her friend's hands over her breast, wiped her own cheeks and left the crib, saddened that she was unable to help, grief stricken at the loss of a friend.

End Notes: Chapter Six

1 Writers have written the legend for years, spelling her name Silver Heels or Silverheels.

2 Archive files of Dr. Nolan Mumey, DPL, and Mrs. Nolan Mumey

3 *Fairplay Flume* files, in particular, the March 1, 1883 edition. This extended research has been included in the reprint of my book, *From the Grave*.

4 Henrietta Denoyer correspondence with author.

5 Mazzulla Files, CHS.

6 The phrase is period slang for transmitting a sexual disease.

7 Mrs. A.H. Majors, *Colorado Magazine*.

8 Fetter, *Telluride*.

SEVEN

"I consider myself then and do now–as a business woman. I operated the best houses in town and I had as my clients the most important men in the West."–Mattie Silks

Soiled Doves Rise Above

"The roaring red light district of the West" is how one writer described Leadville. There has been nothing like the carbonate camp called Leadville, and there never will be. Transportation had come a long way by the time silver made Leadville into the next mining mecca of Colorado in 1878. The town experienced a rush of miners and fortune seekers, ruffs and tuffs, and every sort of human element imaginable. Included in this new influx were the soiled doves, looking for their own opportunity in the new mining camp.

> Lola Daggett, known in Silverton as *"Nigger Lola,"* was not only a beautiful woman, but in time, a respected madam in the community.

Prostitution became part and parcel in a mining camp's "free for all" atmosphere, never more so than in Leadville. Colorful names such as Carrie Linnel, Mollie May, Frankie Paige, Mollie Price, Winnie Purdy, and Sallie Purple reigned supreme in Leadville's tenderloin areas, as high as the city itself.

Leadville, the wildest of the west by many accounts, did not have a designated red light district. State Street was lined with saloons and dance halls. In its heyday, Leadville boasted more than 200 members of the multitude on State Street alone! One such house was owned by Winnie Purdy. The *Leadville Herald Democrat* had the following comment:

> *Paintings that would have sent . . . a preacher into hysterics adorned the walls. Costly furniture, tapestries, velvet carpets, rich Oriental hangings and all the accessories of luxurious elegance were lavished in the interior adornment.*

Winnie Purdy later sold her establishment including all the furnishings to Lillis Lovell, to which the newspaper commented: ". . . one of the most magnificent types of physical womanhood who has played the role of a secumbus in the half world of the Cloud City."[1]

Obviously, Leadville citizens held their courtesans in high esteem. Author Duane Smith was quite correct when he wrote: "Leadville was the only camp which seemed to take real pride in its depravity."[2]

❧ THE PARLOR HOUSES WERE PRIMARILY on Third and Fifth streets. A more elite parlor house, at least by Leadville standards, was located on the southern edge of Leadville's main commerce street, Harrison Avenue.[3] Mollie May's house of ill repute, a two-story frame building across the street and just north of the glorious *Tabor Opera House*, was the place of pleasure for silver king H. A. W. Tabor and his business associates.

Leadville's famous madam, Melinda May Bryant, or Mollie May, as she was known, did extremely well with her various houses and property investments. By the early 1880s, her business was so successful she had relocated to a two-story parlor house on Harrison Avenue. It is said she borrowed the money from H. A. W. Tabor. Within a few years, Mollie sold the house to the city for a new courthouse and made a tidy $10,000 profit.

Generous in her contributions to the town's welfare, including large sums of money to both churches and hospitals, socially Mollie remained an outcast. Yet, the newspapers wrote kindly of her philanthropic deeds. Mollie continued to make headlines.

In the spring of 1882, rumor had it that Mollie was involved in some sort of baby scandal. The rumors, as they often do, turned ugly and cruel. Mollie requested an interview with the *Leadville Herald* newspaper, in an effort to set the record straight. Mollie told the reporter she was simply helping a poor, unfortunate young woman in her time of need. The woman had given birth to a tiny baby, with no means to care for herself or the child. Mollie adopted the baby, so the unfortunate woman could return to her family without shame. Mollie said she gave the woman money for a decent traveling wardrobe and the means to return back East to her family. She went on to tell the reporter she had never refused charitable causes when asked in Leadville, and she would not start now. Evidently this little self-proclamation worked, for Leadville's gossips were silenced.

History does not reveal what became of the baby; however, Mollie soon retired from the bordello business, and led a very quiet secluded life.

At the time of her death in 1887, Mollie had become quite wealthy through her many investments. Her funeral was a grand affair, heavily attended and reported in detail in the Leadville papers. Her eulogy became a lovely poem of endearment:

> *Think of her mournfully,*
> *Sadly, not scornfully-*
> *What she has been is nothing to you.*
> *No one should weep for her,*
> *Now there is sleep for her-*
> *Under the evergreens, daisy and dew.*

> *Talk if you will of her,*
> *But speak no ill of her-*
> *The sins of the living are not of the dead.*
> *Remember her charity,*
> *Forget all disparity;*
> *Let her judges be they whom she sheltered and fed.*

> *Keep her impurity*
> *In dark obscurity,*
> *Only remember the good she has done.*
> *She to the dregs has quaffed*
> *All of life's bitter draught-*
> *Who knows what crown her kindness has won?*

> Though she has been denied,
> The tears of a little child
> May wash from the record much of her sin;
> Whilst others weep and wait
> Outside of Heaven's gate,
> Angels may come to her and lead her in.
>
> When at the judgment throne,
> The master claims his own.
> Dividing the bad from the good and the true.
> There pure and spotless,
> Her rank shall not be less
> Than will be given, perhaps to you.
>
> Then do not sneer at her,
> Or scornfully jeer at her-
> Death came to her, and will come to you.
> Will there be scoffing or weeping,
> When like her, you are sleeping
> Under the evergreens, daisies and dew?

❧ OUR LADIES OF THE TENDERLOIN WERE primarily a strong-willed group of women. They were obstinate, savvy, and courageous. One example is Gussie Blake of Glenwood Springs. John Blake built a house at Bennett and River Front streets for his common law wife, Gussie, who became Glenwood's first madam. She ran a small bordello in the three-room building during the summer of 1885, returning to the East for the winter. In the meantime, Blake rented the building to Garfield County. When Gussie returned in the spring, she found her building occupied. Undaunted, she erected a tented lean-to against the newly constructed court-house, and was soon back in business. The county officials complained in councils, town meetings and the local newspaper, but to no avail. Gussie was within her legal rights. Gussie remained at this location for over a year, when a house was built for her, reportedly by the city, on Cooper Avenue. Gussie remained in business for several years, and retired in a comfortable style.

In Lake City, Bluff Street, located on the west side of town at the base of the mountain, was the red light district that at one time was known as *Hell's Acres*.

Bluff Street was a popular attraction for the local miners. And no one was more popular than Clara Ogden. Clara arrived during the booming years of the mining town and set out to improve the image, in her own curious way. Clara bought a large lot on Bluff Street, tore out the dingy cribs and built the *Crystal Palace*. The magnificent two-story bordello contained a large ballroom on the first floor, with walnut detailing, mirrors, and chandeliers. The second floor included a large number of rooms.

For more than twenty years, Clara Ogden was the queen of Lake City's red light district. In 1895, Clara looked to expand her operation to nearby smaller mining camps. She bought a lovely painted carriage pulled by matching bay horses. Every few weeks Clara and a few of her girls would dress in their finest outfits and take a carriage ride to the outlining mining camps. Smiling and waving, it made for good advertising for Clara's *Crystal Palace*.

Madam Susie Brown of Boulder, didn't give up on her bordello business at 1045 Water Street, although she was burned out seven times! She finally built a brick two-story building at Eighteenth and Spruce streets where her business continued for several years.

In Durango, a well-known madam named Betty ran her popular parlor house for years following prohibition. When America entered World War II, Betty sold her business and joined the armed forces. She later became a captain in the WACS.[4]

Lola Daggett was a Silverton prostitute who lived out her lively days and serene old age in one place. Born and raised in Pueblo, Lola and her sister Freda headed for the San Juans arriving in Silverton in 1905.

The two sisters operated a crib on Blair Street and were fairly successful until Freda died in 1912, at the age of thirty-five.

Lola continued her prostitution profession and eventually saved enough money to purchase a bordello at 1135 Blair Street. She employed two to three girls and soon had a very popular establishment.

Because Lola was a black woman, she was known as "Nigger" Lola in turn of the century Silverton. Undaunted, Lola's business did so well that she bought a second bordello, with the finest furnishings and first class service, including a black *female* piano player. Lola ran a fine establishment and gained a good measure of respect along the row. So much so, that a long standing rumor held that a distinguished town attorney secretly left his home and family nightly, to be with Lola.

Years later, "Jew Fanny," another Silverton lady of the evening, confided to a friend that she watched the attorney enter Lola's house *almost every night.*

Lola did very well in her business. She bought herself a fine fur coat and several automobiles over the years, although she did not drive. Perhaps owing to her great sense of humor, Lola hired a white man to drive her wherever she wanted to go. And so, Lola became a beloved citizen of Silverton. She contributed to charities, baked cakes and pies for the sick, and handed out her home-made candy to children.

Lola's health deteriorated rapidly and by 1937, she was forced to sell her business. A friend and business owner named Rose Stewart took Lola into her home, where she remained until her death in November 1939. Honest and loyal to the end, Lola's will left what little she had to Rose Stewart.

She's the kind of girl who climbed the ladder of
success wrong by wrong. — Mae West

Bessie Rivers was Durango's leading madam. A late arrival by local standards she appeared when Durango had settled into a respectable town. Nevertheless, her arrival turned heads.

Bessie set up for business at 969 Main Avenue, one of Durango's two tenderloin districts. Not a shy woman or timid for that matter, she advertised quite openly, hired girls and soon opened her business. Her bordello was the most popular in town, and in time, Bessie made a name for herself. Of course, Bessie Rivers wasn't her real name; most prostitutes changed their names for a variety of reasons. Yet, Bessie is a figure in Durango history that is still talked about today.

Bessie's parlor house, known as the *Horseshoe Saloon*, was typical of most saloons in Durango, at least in appearance. What set the Horseshoe apart was Bessie's flair for elegance and her flair for opulence. The atmosphere at Bessie's was always gay, full of music, fine food, and elegant wines. Five-course meals often featured oysters on the half shell, fresh fruits, and vintage wines, all served by candlelight. This fine meal and entertainment would be served with an extra flair: in Bessie's plush and very private suite, located on the floor above. Furnished in extravagant, thick rugs, velvet curtains, imported furniture, and soft lighting, the rooms must have been a sight to behold. Dinner was served on fine china, with rare wine, all brought upstairs to Bessie's quarters by a dumb-waiter.

At the back end of the *Horseshoe Saloon* was the kitchen and a detached dance hall. An arched design carved into the brick entrance also faced the alley way (today's Narrow Gauge Avenue). Opposite the long bar, benches were set up where Bessie's girls sat, waiting for a dance. The dance floor, narrow, yet long, was in the middle of the room. Music was provided by a small band, or a hired piano player. As the girls danced, arrangements were made for "other activities" with their dance partners, and with a prearranged nod to the manager, the girls would lead their customers to the rooms above.

It was Bessie's practice of being fair and honest that endeared her to both her customers and Durango businessmen. Oftentimes, the area miners, some as far away as Silverton, would come to Durango for fun and relaxation. At Bessie's place, they would pay in gold, gold dust, or silver. This was not an unusual practice for miners; however at Bessie's, she required the customer to turn over all the ore in whatever form to the house for safekeeping. When the customer was ready to leave, the valuables were returned, less the expenses due during the customer's stay. This method ruled out robbery and gained the customer's confidence.

Bessie Rivers earned a fine business reputation throughout the town, despite her profession. She invested in many business properties in and around Durango. She was also well-known for her many acts of charity. She solicited donations from the other bordellos in town for the various causes in Durango. A particular favorite of Bessie's was a college fund she instigated through one of the local banks.

Bessie finally retired in 1925. She bought a charming frame home at 3310 Main Avenue, a very nice section of town. There she lived quite comfortably, tending her garden and attending very few social engagements. Her home still stands today, although a very altered version.

Years later, Bessie moved back into her *Horseshoe Saloon* at 969 Main Avenue, which she still owned. She died in 1937. She was buried in the stately Greenmount Cemetery. The small tombstone gives her real name, Frankie Fergeson, not known in life, except to a few. Bessie, (or Frankie,) left behind collectible pieces of antiques, silver, and china. What cannot be collected, only remembered and recorded for history, is the great legacy she left for Durango that is very much a part of Durango's past, spoken of today with much admiration.

The *Georgetown Courier* of March 22, 1882, reported the monetary accomplishments of Cordelia Santee:

Silver was discovered in Oro Gulch and Leadville became the mecca for all society, not the least of which were the ladies of the prostitution trade. Leadville claimed not one but three separate red light sections in the wicked city.

Obviously one of the finest parlor houses in Leadville. Could one of these women be Lillis Lovell, Mollie May, or Sally Purple?

Elizabeth Marshall, known as "Cockeyed Liz," because of an inflicted punch to the eye, later became a respected married woman in Buena Vista. She is shown at her home with two young visitors.

Denver's Queen of the Row, Mattie Silks, (left) retired in Denver with her beloved prized horses.

Dorothy Brown, known in Silverton as "Tar Baby," was a mulatto prostitute who found happiness after years of degradation and racism. She died in 1971, the last of Colorado's Legends in Lace.

Cordelia Santee, well-known among many Georgetown mashers and smashers, is getting considerable notoriety through the newspapers. She roped in and married Norman J. Fillmore, at Denver, a prospective heir to half a million. After he found out whom he had married, he demanded a divorce, and gave her $5,000 to keep her mouth shut until it could be procured. She is quite willing he should have his divorce for the modest consideration of $75,000 and the probabilities are she will get the money. Then there will be an opportunity for some of her Georgetown flames to try their luck for a wife with a fortune.

As famous or infamous as many of Colorado's courtesans may have been, only one of these women made national headlines. Verona Baldwin came to Denver fresh from California and scandal.

Verona's cousin, E. J. "Lucky" Baldwin worked his way up, starting as a livery boy during the Comstock boom in Nevada, to become one of the wealthiest land owners in California. He owned the luxurious Baldwin Hotel in San Francisco and one of the nation's finest horse racing tracks. He brought twenty year-old Verona to his California ranch where she originally taught school. All seemed normal until the *San Francisco Call* on January 5, 1883, exploded the following headline before all the world:

A WOMAN'S REVENGE
Lucky Baldwin Shot by His Young Cousin, Verona

According to the article and subsequent police and court documents, Verona was immediately arrested. At police headquarters, learning the shot to her cousin's arm was not serious, she said, "I ought to have killed him. I did not try to kill him. I hit him just where I wanted to, for I am a good shot and never miss anything I aim at." She said Baldwin had ruined her in body and mind.

He had raped her, she said, then framed her by bringing charges against her which resulted in her dismissal from the school. In court testimony, she alluded to being a witness to an illegal land deal. Baldwin's attorney claimed illicit sexual favors on the part of Verona as the cause for her dismissal.

In any case, the trial never occurred, for Lucky refused to testify and Verona was acquitted. However, three years later, Verona made headlines again when she threatened to sue Lucky for child support for her child she claimed was Lucky's. No suit materialized, but the scandal was far from over. A few years later, Verona was again before a court judge where she was determined to be insane and sent to an asylum. According to an attorney from Los Angles, her stay was brief and without medical cause, and probably instigated by Lucky Baldwin.

Shortly before the turn of the century, Verona Baldwin had made her way east to Denver. Described as nearly six feet tall, slender and beautiful, with large hazel green eyes, Verona possessed a soft English accent and a presence that made her queen-like in many circles. She even claimed to be a member of British royalty.

However, English culture was not on Verona's mind when she took over a Market Street establishment 1897. Evidently Verona ran a respectable business, as the *Rocky Mountain News* of April 28, 1898, reported:

> *Saved from a Life of Vice*
> *A pretty blue eyed young woman arrived in the city . . . intending to seek employment. A woman at the employment office advised her to adopt a course of vise . . . Tuesday night the woman, called "Mary Anderson," in company with a notorious procuress, rang the bell of a brothel, where she was referred to another dive. At the latter place arrangements were quickly completed. In less than an hour, the landlady was informed that the girl was innocent. The landlady, Verona Baldwin . . . pleaded with the girl for the sake of mother and family to return to her home. Verona Baldwin called the police . . . and later she was taken to Union Station to catch a train to a relative's home. The police paid for the ticket.*[5]

By 1903, Verona purchased a parlor house at 2020 Market Street, once owned by Lillis Lovell, and with her reputation and business acumen, turned her establishment into one of the finest. Not only did she have a head for business, as well as a good heart, in appearance, she outclassed the dominating Mattie Silks and the pretty Jennie Rogers.

Verona dressed in the most elegant fashions of the day and made them her own personal statement. She always wore velvet, usually purple, but she also wore gold or red and always accented in lace. Her premature gray hair was always worn up, in the fashion of the day, and topped with a jeweled tiara. Her manners were impeccable and dignified.

Verona's house of pleasure did quite well and for a time threatened other establishments on Market Street, including Mattie's and Jennie's houses of ill repute. Verona was quite a wealthy woman when the good citizens for reform began to make strides among Denver's society. Verona's establishment catered to the "more esteemed" clientele of Denver and survived the reformation for a time.

When prostitution was "officially" shut down, Verona Baldwin sold her house on Market Street and bought a hotel near Denver's capitol hill area, known as *The Baldwin Inn*. Verona operated the successful hotel until her death in the 1940s. Her estate was said to be considerable.

Buffalo Gals Won't You Come Out Tonight

Following the war with Mexico, Sarah Borginnis accompanied the soldiers during expeditions in California. It is said she was admired by the soldiers for her strength and work ethic. Sarah has been described as nearly six feet tall, with red hair and blue eyes. At night, she showed her kindness to the soldiers in a different way. Sarah made a practice of following soldiers in times of war.

Born in Tennessee in 1813, Sarah worked as a cook with the Missouri 7th Infantry. In Texas, she kept kettles of soup and hot coffee ready as the soldiers fought the Mexicans at Fort Brown.

At a skirmish near Saltillo, Texas, Sarah nursed the wounded and helped to keep the supply lines open. At one point, a hysterical soldier rode in to camp, reporting of the dead and wounded. It is said Sarah jerked the soldier off the horse, telling him to get a hold of himself, for if he spread such a report to the camp troops, she would personally beat him to death.

Following the war, Sarah bought property in the new town of Colorado City, living a respectable life for a few years. Sarah visited Texas again in 1866, where she died and was given a fine military funeral.

Happily Ever After

While the percentages are low, a few soiled doves did endure to go on to enjoy happier lives. Many married and some even had families.

Mary Scheidt owned one of Silverton's early bordellos. Within fifteen years, Mary married a local shoe maker, had a child and retired to a life of homemaking.

Georgetown, with its silver riches, attracted all types of humanity, including soiled doves. One frail sister arrived from the East in 1877. She dressed well, spoke well, and carried an air of refinement about her. It is not surprising that, when she joined the bordello of madam Lotted White, the citizens of Georgetown were aghast. Miners who favored the prostitute called her "Tidbit," perhaps because of her small stature. In any case, she was popular in Georgetown.

Within a few months, another distinguished-looking lady from the East got off the train at Georgetown. The woman's first stop was the police station. There, she explained she was looking for her sister, who had fled from her abusive husband and their home town. The police escorted the woman to Lotted White's bordello, where "Tidbit" was reunited with her sister. The sisters cried joyous tears at the reunion and soon left Georgetown forever. It is said that "Tidbit" obtained a divorce, led a respectful life and later remarried, happily.

Rose Lane began her career as a hurdy-gurdy girl in Silverton. Unlike most soiled doves who eventually moved from town to town, Rose stayed in Silverton for her entire career, which spanned decades. She occupied her own crib on Blair Street until the Silverton city council shut down businesses on the infamous street following World War II. Rose married Carl Blake, a mining blacksmith, and the two left Silverton for Oklahoma, where they bought a ranch.

Elizabeth Marshall arrived in Buena Vista in 1886.[6] Her fancy dress and painted face told the town her trade. In no time, she acquired a lot on the north side of Main Street, where she built a one-story brick house. Lizzie, as she came to be called, opened the finest parlor house within a one hundred miles of Buena Vista. Liz's place boasted a formal room, a parlor, four girls, music, and servants. Known as the *Palace of Joy*, Lizzie's bordello became the popular attraction throughout the town. So popular was Liz's place that rival madam, Belle Brown, conspired to rid the town of Lizzie. Brown's vicious assault left Lizzie blind in one eye and with the loss of muscle control, thereby earning her the new name of "Cock-eyed Liz." The aftermath of the assault endeared Liz to most of the town's citizens, while Belle Brown was forced to leave town.

Liz has been described as fairly tall, over five feet and seven inches, dark brown hair and blue eyes, fair skinned and beautiful. One of her many customers was a plumber by the name of Alphonse Enderlin, a native of France. Known as "Foozy" around town, he was a kind, good natured fellow who seemed to enjoy spending his free time at Liz's Palace of Joy.

Foozy enjoyed working in Liz's garden and making wine in her kitchen. Liz enjoyed his company and soon, romance became the natural way between the two. On a fall day in 1897, Liz and Foozy were married during an overnight trip to Fairplay. The happy couple returned to Buena Vista and Liz's house, where Foozy took over the household duties. Gone were Liz's girls; apartments were added for steady "legal" income, and Liz became a housewife. The marriage was a happy one for over thirty years. The couple traveled, entertained friends, and supported the community.

Cock-eyed Liz, one-time madam, died in 1929 from a weakened heart, followed by Foozy five years later, from a broken heart.

Several members of the multitude survived their early colorful life to live quite happily in their golden years.

In 1880, Mattie Silks bought a nice home in a fashionable residential area of Denver, 2635 Lawrence Street. She would maintain this house until her death in 1929. It was also about this time that Mattie began the first of some twenty purchases of thoroughbred horses. It seems even in retirement, Mattie lived a racy life until the end.

Another member of Silverton's tenderloin, was madam Jane Bowen. Jane owned two separate bordellos, and in time, acquired considerable wealth. During the 1890s, Jane suffered a number of personal tragedies including the deaths of her adopted daughter, and a nephew who had been living with her. Somehow, Jane managed to keep her business running strong. However, by 1898, she leased out her last bordello and left Silverton for her native home of England, where she lived in comfort, returning to America and particularly Silverton, for extended visits.

Leadville madam Winnie Purdy gained a measure of respect and moderate popularity during the 1880s. There is some speculation regarding Winnie's later years. She returned to the East for a short time in 1884, and leased one of her Leadville bordellos to Lillis Lovell. She returned to Leadville for a few years, probably in the latter part of 1885, eventually selling one of her properties to Lillis in 1887. Eventually, Winnie Purdy moved to the East permanently and retired very comfortably.

Fanny Wright, known as "Jew Fanny" on Silverton's Blair Street, was the last of the soiled doves in southwestern Colorado. Fanny continued to work at the *National Hall* saloon and bordello in the 1940s, when several Hollywood westerns were filmed on the streets of Silverton. While the *National Hall* received a face lift for the Hollywood films, Fanny continued to ply her trade inside, only to be forced into retirement due to her age. She continued to live in a small room at the *National Hall* until her death.

Amazing Grace...

The life of the soiled dove was typically not a pretty one. Yet, these women found a way to endure, and many did.

Frances Daws, a soiled dove of Market Street, found herself out of work when reform took hold in 1916. In time, Frances found religion, joined a church, and preached the gospel in lower downtown Denver.

When Laura Allman was arrested for prostitution in 1904, she cried hysterically. Eventually, she was able to recount her life story to the arresting officer, who later contacted the media.[7] Laura's story is a sad one, as is typical of many soiled doves. However, the ending is a happy one.

Orphaned as a child, Laura went to work in a cotton mill on Evans Avenue in northwest Denver. A laborer at a nearby brick yard soon won her over, and the two were married. The marriage was a bad one from the start. Laura's husband drank constantly and soon lost his job at the brick yard. Expecting Laura to provide the income, he quickly found a second job for her. As mounting debt became unmanageable, an overwhelmed Laura went to work at the crib job her husband had obtained for her. "Something had to be done to keep us from starving," she said.

Laura thought often of suicide, but held out hope that things would get better. Shortly after her arrest, her husband and a couple of his friends were arrested for murder.

Laura was then assigned to a police matron, where arrangements were made for her "rescue from a life of shame."

"Denver Kate," as she was known in the tenderloin district of Silverton, occupied a three-room crib near the southeast corner of 12th Street and Blair Street for the majority of her working years.[8] In her later years, she shared a log cabin with Molly Foley, another well-known madam of the district. The two conducted a laundry service for the girls on Blair Street. "Denver Kate" died at the age of seventy-eight, in 1925. She had managed her prostitute earnings to pay for college at the University of Colorado for both of her daughters, who never knew what she did for a living.

Molly Foley died in 1914. Known throughout the town of Silverton as difficult, hard to work for, and a trouble maker, not to mention an alcoholic and drug abuser, the *Silverton Standard* of January 2, 1915, had this to say:

The death of Molley Foley, which occurred last Tuesday evening, marked the passing of one of the most notorious characters known to the San Juan district. She came here thirty-six years ago after an eventful career in Chama, Animas City, Durango, and many of the early frontier camps. She was formally noted for her vivacity, neatness of dress and generosity. To those who knew her in late years, crippled and dejected, it would be hard to recognize any of the charms that made her attractive in the days of the prairie schooners. She was about seventy-eight years of age, and left no known relatives. The funeral was held Thursday from McCleod's undertaking parlors.

The *Rocky Mountain News* of January 23, 1884, reported the death of Mattie Estes in a very respectful light, unusual for the times.

Today will occur the burial of Mattie Estes, late of Georgetown, Colo., who died a few days ago in New Orleans, wither she had gone for her health, being afflicted with paralysis. The deceased was a noted member of the demimonde, (sic) and acquired quite a large fortune through her disreputable avocation, which she willed to her solid man, named King. She was about 60 years of age. Unlike the majority of her class about whom post mortem yarns are related, it is reasonably safe to say that she never was a member of any highly respectable family. From all that can be learned of her, she was wealthy and carried on her business with a design to realizing the largest possible returns, quite peculiar to the early days of Colorado.

Dorothy Brown's life is one of sadness and miserable endurance. The very fact that she lived to be eighty-two years old shows inner strength at the very least.

Born in Chicago in 1889, Dorothy was sent to an orphanage. A mulatto, Dorothy was an unwanted child. She left Chicago and her unhappy childhood after the turn of the century. Still a teenager, Dorothy went into the prostitution trade in Silverton. For the most part, she worked in cribs, where she was commonly known as "Tar Baby," a hideous reference to her heritage.

By her own account, she was in trouble often, once remarking how many times she had spent time in Silverton's jail. It is said she started just as many fights as she ended and ". . . could hold her own against just about anyone."

After Silverton closed down Blair Street's prostitution trade, Dorothy married Frank Brown, a native of Silverton and a retired sheriff. The couple moved to the south section of town, where they lived for many years.

Dorothy died in February of 1971, truly the last of our tenderloin ladies.

❧ Some legends never seem to die, nor can they be proven or disproven. Perhaps legends can serve a useful purpose. Such is the case of Red Stockings, for this legend gave a sense of hope to many prostitutes in the cold, dirty, lonely mining camps of Colorado's Rocky Mountains.

Red Stockings, so named for the color of the leggings she wore to keep warm, was among the first of the prostitutes to reach the new gold diggings of the 1859 gold rush to Colorado's mountains. In early 1860, she settled in California Gulch, a narrow canyon high in mountain terrain rich in ore, and where a full fifteen years later, the richest silver strike would cause Leadville to become a legend in itself. However, in 1860, the allure was gold; a rush of some 5,000 fortune seekers swarmed the tiny gulch. Trees fell as structures were hastily built to accommodate the onslaught.

Red Stockings reportedly had a small cabin, and as the only prostitute in the camp, she obviously did a great business. Her real name is long forgotten, if ever known, but it is said she was a beauty (aren't they all?) As the legend goes, she came from a wealthy eastern family, got into some sort of sinful trouble and fled west to escape her past and save her family from shame. In any case, Red Stockings became the darling of California Gulch. Two years later, as the legend goes, she had accomplished what she came west for: money and lots of it.

Red Stockings allegedly threw a party for the miners and said goodbye to them, the mining camp, Colorado and prostitution. With thousands of dollars, she left Colorado, settled back east, or further west, depending on which version of the legend one believes, and became a respectable woman, eventually marrying.

A legend, an inspiration, or a fanciful dream? It mattered not to the soiled doves who believed.

End Notes: Chapter Seven

1 *Leadville Herald Democrat*

2 Smith, *Rocky Mountain Mining Camp*

3 Blair, *Leadville: Colorado's Magic City*

4 Jarvis, *Come on in Dearie.*

5 *Rocky Mountain News*, April 28, 1898.

6 Tax records reveal her name as Elizabeth Marshall, later changed to Elizabeth Enderlin.

7 *Rocky Mountain News*, February 2, 1904.

8 Bird, *Bordellos of Blair Street.*

EPILOGUE

"You can't sell it when they're given it away for free."
– "Jew Fanny"

Our ladies of the tenderloin left a colorful history in Colorado, a legend in lace. Prostitution was a notable trade in Colorado simply because it was an important aspect of social life in towns and mining camps across the state. Saloons, dance halls, and bordellos were the center of society in many communities during the early years. Women were the center of these establishments, and women, despite or because of their station in the early frontier, helped make Colorado the colorful state it is.

As the reform movement gained momentum, prostitution no longer held its notable domain, yet it did not disappear into the night . . . for a time. The sexual need of the male population was still there. The economic theory of supply and demand applied, as well as the revenue generated for local government from taxes, fees, and fines.

With the taming of the West came changes. Respectability, stable lifestyles, family values — in short — civilized society.

The changes in moral behavior did not come easy. Indeed, it took decades. Reform began in the East, and slowly made its way West, where it seemed to ebb and flow for several years.

The prostitution influence in the West was a direct reflection of the lack of women in the region. By this very virtue, prostitutes were a needed and desired commodity. The fact that prostitution remained a viable commodity, despite the later presence of women of moral virtue, speaks more to Victorian platitudes than to the prostitutes of the West.

In due time, women gained strength, if only in numbers, and reform was soon on the horizon. Yet, our ladies of the tenderloin showed they could, in fact, fight city hall. From Durango to Denver, these women not only protested, but forced many city officials to back down. Mattie and Jennie, who led their Market Street girls in downtown Denver, dressed for combat in yellow from head to toe and forced city officials to rescind their ridiculous yellow banded prostitution stamp. The ordinance, meant to denigrate the prostitutes, marked Denver's city officials for the nincompoops they were.

In towns across Colorado, law enforcement hardly fared any better. Revenue from licensing and fines for prostitution helped pay for government. Lawmen were oftentimes deciding whether to wink or collect. One old timer remarked, "How do you think Silverton got these fine sidewalks?" In Cripple Creek, Marshal Wilson endeavored to keep the peace in his town by moving "the line" one block south of town.

Perhaps the words of Ernest Hoffman correctly convey the attitude of many Colorado citizens in the early stages of reform:

My dad bought a boarding house in Silverton in the early 1900s and boarded only miners. He lost his butt because the boarding house was the last place the miners paid. As soon as they hit town they would head for Blair Street and blow all their money on gambling and women. As for the women, they were a social necessity in those days. You've got to remember that almost all of the miners in those days were young and single. After spending three or four months up at the mine they just had to get away for a break. Of course they never got past Silverton. Silverton was wide open with gambling and women 24 hours a day. There were a lot of "do-gooders' in town that wanted to do away with the women but Joe Terry and the other mine managers fought to keep them. It was important that the men remained in good spirits and the gambling and women served that purpose.[1]

When Robert W. Speer became mayor of Denver in 1904, he immediately adopted a "no stance" stance regarding the many attempts at reform in Denver.

No effort will be made to make a puritanical town of a growing western city. An administration should always stand for what is right, but you must take the people as you find them. Vice will not run riot, but wherever found will be promptly controlled or suppressed. Social evils that cannot be abolished will be restricted and regulated so as to do the least possible harm.

In short, Speer figured if he stayed neutral, his political future would be ensured; he could always take a position later. In this manner, Speer appeared to be letting the matter run its course. Many Colorado cities followed his example.

When Carrie Nation reeled her booze-hating ax in Denver, she walked Market Street, screaming hateful comments at the soiled doves:

You poor, degraded wretch, I pity you. I have hatred for you. You are the victim of bad, bad men, rotten heredity, and a terrible environment. The police are living off you. How much do you have to pay every month to continue your awful life of sin?

Denver police officers arrived and hauled Nation off in a paddy wagon.[2]

Yet, the reform movement could not be stopped. It was time for change. And so it was with prostitution in the West. In the end, national prohibition, rather than reform, was the final blow to a bygone era.

The final crackdown on Denver bordellos began in 1913. Prohibition became law in Colorado in 1916, a full three years before the nation went "dry."

By 1916, most red light districts across Colorado had turned out their lights forever. It was the end of an era. Victorian parlor houses, once gay and filled with music, laughter and ball gowns, were becoming industrial warehouses.

Durango fought Prohibition with all its might. As with all towns across Colorado, and the nation, for that matter, establishments in the entertainment business were greatly effected by the national ban of liquor. Bootlegging was the result. Many Durango businessmen pooled their resources and bought railroad carloads of grapes from California, all quite legally. What they did with the grapes, of course, was not legal. But for a time, Durango establishments, including the bordellos, enjoyed a very fine, yet strong, dry red wine.

Again, Ernest Hoffman of Silverton wisely described the effects of prohibition in his town:

After prohibition came, the gals sold bootleg booze along with the bars. The city fathers soon got wise to the fact that this was a ripe source of revenue. Each bootlegger and girl on the line had to come in each month and pay a set fine. That's how all those cement sidewalks were built. The girls could only go to Main Street to shop and pick up their mail. They were never allowed to linger there. One merchant that sold fine ladieswear (sic) made a fortune off of those girls.[3]

When America entered World War I, military bases across Colorado became automatic destinations for many soiled doves. Conversely, military personnel on leave often headed for known bordellos still in operation, such as Miss Laura's place in Salida, or Miss Lil's in Florence. Evidently, soldiers were good for business as Miss Laura Evans and Miss Lillian Powers were the only grand "old" madams to maintain their business operations until the early 1950s, when each died of old age.

Following Prohibition and the Roaring Twenties, in which prostitution received a short reprieve, a new social atmosphere emerged. For years reformers, and even politicians, had protested against the sins of vice in their particular town. Over the years, their efforts paid off, little by little. Yet, to our ladies credit, they defended their profession with true veracity. By the twentieth century, neither the city officials nor law enforcement could appease the growing public opinion for change. One newspaper commentator remarked upon the closing of red light districts:

> . . . yesterday a riotous sector of the demimonde, housing its courtesans and their ilk, bounded on the north by stumbling virtue, on the south by wrecked hopes, on the east by the miserably gray dawn of shame and on the west by the sunset of dissipation. — Gene Fowler

Reform had settled the dusty wild ways of yesteryear. Still, prostitution continued in some form throughout World War II, as it does today.

Today, there is sentiment, understanding, and a deep curiosity for the ladies and their nineteenth century haunts.

In Salida, near the train station, Laura Evans' house still stands, now apartments. Just to the west, a mountain is named for Silver Heels. Leadville's State Street, as well as Silverton's Blair Street, are well marked on tourists maps, and complete with walking tours and a brief history. Denver's Market Street still exists. Bordellos that became warehouses or storage facilities are now being reborn in the fabulous *Lo Do* area, complete with the history of the original businesses. In Cripple Creek, the *Homestead House* is now a museum.

From the lamplight ladies, to the madams of the row, from their successes to their tragedies, these women are part of history . . . a part of a bygone era, to be sure, yet an era rich in nostalgia.

Our ladies of the tenderloin's heyday in the American West was relatively brief. From cow town beginnings to mining booms and busts, the soiled doves provided what was then considered to be a necessary commodity that has slowly disappeared.

No matter what one's opinion may be, it cannot be denied: these women, as a whole, had the fortitude to persevere regardless of circumstances.

Yet, a way of life, once vital to the early economy of hundreds of struggling towns across Colorado, has a place in the history of the state.

History has been kind to *Our Ladies of the Tenderloin*.

End Notes: Epilogue

1 Bird, *Bordellos of Blair Street*.
2 *The Denver Post*, August 12, 1906.
3 Bird, *Bordellos of Blair Street*.

END OF THE LINE

Name	Died	Burial Site
Bassett, Amy	1904	Fairmount Cemetery
Borginnis, Sarah	1866	Saltillo, Texas
Brock, Anna	1883	Leadville *
Brown, Mabel	1903	Riverside Cemetery, Denver
Burton, Blanche	1909	Colorado City
Chambers, Fannie	1884	Aspen
Contassot, Marie	1894	Riverside Cemetery, Denver
DeVere, Pearl	1897	Cripple Creek
Doyle, Sadie	1950	Mount Olivet Cemetery, Denver
Enderlin, Elizabeth (Cock-eyed Liz)		
	1929	Buena Vista
Evans, Laura	1953	Salida
Fergeson, Frankie (Bessie Rivers)		
	1937	Durango
Landers, Jessie	1900	Lake City *
Lovell, Lillis	1907	Cremation, Riverside Cemetery
Lovell, Lois	1908	Riverside Cemetery, Denver
May, Mollie	1887	Leadville
Moore, Effie	1887	Riverside Cemetery, Denver *
Powers, Lillian	1960	Pennsylvania
Rogers, Jennie	1909	Fairmount Cemetery, Denver
Russell, Nellie	1892	Creede
Silks, Mattie	1929	Fairmount Cemetery, Denver
Walker, Mabel	1899	Telluride
Wellington, Ella	1894	Riverside Cemetery, Denver

*Unmarked grave

Bibliography

Unpublished Works including Records, Diaries, Papers and Manuscripts

Denoyer, Henrietta, writings and personal papers regarding Laura Evans.

Howe, Sam. Scrapbooks, Colorado Historical Society.

Jarvis, Marion, *"Come on in Dearie"* copy from Fort Lewis College Center of South West Studies.

Mumey, Nolie personal papers and collections including notes on interviews, Denver Public Library, Western History Collection.

Shores, Cyrus W, manuscript and personal papers, Denver Public Library, Western History Collection.

City, County, State, and Government Records

Colorado State Archives

Colorado State Penitentiary Records

Denver City and County Public Records

Gilpin County Records

Silverton Town Hall Records and Ordinance Archives

Newspapers, Articles & Archives

Carbonate Weekly Chronicle (Leadville)

Colorado City Independent

Colorado City Iris

Colorado Miner (Georgetown)

Creed Candle

Daily Miner's Register (Central City)

Denver Post

Durango Herald

Fairplay Flume

Georgetown Courier

Gunnison Review

Lake City Silver World

LaPlata Miner (Silverton)

Leadville Daily Chronicle (Leadville)

Leadville Daily Democrat (Leadville)

Leadville Daily Herald (Leadville)

Leadville Evening Chronicle

Leadville Weekly Herald (Leadville)

Red Mountain Pilot (Red Mountain)

Register Call (Central City)

Rocky Mountain News (Denver)

Rocky Mountain Sun (Aspen)

Silverton Democrat (Silverton)

Solid Muldoon (Ouray)

    Colorado Magazine, November 1945 – "Life in North Creede in the Early Days", Mrs. A.H. Majors

Books

Bancroft, Caroline, *Six Racy Madams of Colorado*. Johnson Publishing 1965.

Bates, Margaret, *A Quick History of Lake City Colorado*. Little London Press 1973.

Bird, Allan G. *Bordellos of Blair Street*. The Other Shop 1987.

Blair, Edward, *Leadville: Colorado's Magic City*. Pruett Publishing 1980.

Blair, Kay Reynolds, *Ladies of the Lamplight*. Self Published 1971.

Butler, Anne M, *Daughters of Joy, Sisters of Misery*. University of Illinois Press, 1985.

Carter, Louis J. *Yesterday Was Another Day*. St. James Methodist Church publication 1989.

Couch, Jacqualine Grannell, *Those Golden Girls of Market Street*. Old Army Press 1974.

Dallas, Sandra, *Cherry Creek Gothic*. University of Oklahoma Press 1971.

Feitz, Leland, *Myers Avenue, A Quick History*. Little London Press 1967.

Feitz, Leland, *A Quick History of Creede* . Little London Press 1969.

Fetter, Richard L. and Suzanne C., *Telluride: From Pick to Powder*. Caxton Printers 1979.

Fowler, Gene, *A Solo in Tom-Toms*. Viking Press 1946.

Goldstein, Phil, *The Seamy Side of Denver*. Denver New Social Publications 1993.

Granruth, Alan, *A Guide To Downtown Central City, Colorado*. Self published 1989.

Griswold, Don and Griswold, Jean, *History of Leadville and Lake County, Colorado*. University Press of Colorado 1996.

Houston, Grant, *Lake City Reflections* B & B Printers 1976.

Jeffery, Julie Roy, *Frontier Women; The Trans-Mississippi West 1840-1880*. Hill and Wang 1979.

Jessen, Kenneth, *Colorado Gunsmoke*. Pruett Publishing 1986.

Jessen, Kenneth, *Georgetown: A Quick History*. First Light Publishing 1996.

Mazzulla, Fred and Mazzulla, Jo, *Brass Checks and Red Lights*. Self published 1966.

Miller, Max with Mazulla, Fred *Holladay Street*. Ballantine Books 1962.

Miller, Ronald Dean, *Shady Ladies of the West*. Westernlore Press 1964.

Mumey, Nolie, *Calamity Jane*. The Range Press 1950.

Mumey, Nolie *Creede :A History of a Colorado Silver Mining Town* .Artcraft Press 1949.

Noel, Thomas J. *The City and the Saloon*. University of Nebraska Press 1982.

Noel, Thomas J. *Denver's Larimer Street*. Historic Denver 1981.

Parkhill, Forbes, *The Wildest of the West*. Henry Holt and Company 1951.

Reiter, Joan Swallow, *The Women*. Time Life Books 1979.

Rohrbough, Malcolm J. *Aspen*. New York Oxford University Press 1986.

Secrest, Clark, *Hell's Belles: Denver's Brides of the Multitude*. Hindsight Historical Publications 1996.

Seagraves, Anne, *Soiled Doves ,Prostitution in the Early West*. Wasanne 1994.

Smith, Duane, *Durango Diary*. The Herald Press 1996.

Smith, Duane, *Rocky Mountain Mining Camps*. University Press of Colorado, 1992.

Shikes, Robert L. *Rocky Mountain Medicine* . Johnson Books 1986.

Sprague, Marshall *Money Mountain*. University of Nebraska Press 1953.

West, Elliot, *The Saloon on the Rocky Mountain Mining Frontier*. University of Nebraska Press 1979.

Urquhart, Lena M. *Roll Call, The Violent and Lawless*. Golden Bell Press, 1967.

Wommack, Linda, *From The Grave*. Caxton Press 1998.

INTERVIEWS AND CORRESPONDENCE

Denoyer, Henrietta, San Diego, CA

Dougal, Cliff, Riverside Cemetery

Granruth, Alan, Gilpin County Historical Society

Hughes, David, Old Colorado History Center

Jones, Linda, President, Gilpin County Historical Society

Lindsey, Daryl, Florence Chamber of Commerce

Muney, Mrs. Nolan

Noel, Professor Thomas J., Denver University

Smith, Professor Duane, Fort Lewis College, Durango

Stephens, Maggie, Fort Morgan Museum

INDEX

THE AUTHOR

L inda Wommack is a Colorado native who has enjoyed Colorado history since childhood. She is a distant relative of Bob Womack, the man who discovered gold at Cripple Creek. Linda has published several books dealing with the history of the state, including *Our Ladies of the Tenderloin, From the Grave: A Roadside Guide to Colorado's Pioneer Cemeteries, Colorado Gambling: A History of the Early Days, Cripple Creek Tailings* and *Colorado History for Kids*. Linda's articles have appeared in *The Casino Player, The Tombstone Epitaph, The American Epitaph, True West Magazine, The Gold Prospector* and *American Western Magazine*.

Other books
about Colorado
From *Caxton Press*

From the Grave:
A Roadside Guide to Colorado's Pioneer Cemeteries
6 x 9, 500 pages, 100 photos
ISBN 0-87004-386-2, paper, $24.95
ISBN 0-87004-390-0, cloth, $34.95

Colorado Treasure Tales
ISBN 0-87004-402-8 $13.95
6 x 9, 200 pages, maps, bibliography, $14.95

Pioneers of the Colorado Parks
ISBN 0-87004-381-1
6x9, 276 pages, paper, $17.95

Colorado Ghost Towns
Past and Present
ISBN 0-87004-218-1
6x9, 322 pages, map, photographs, paper, $14.95

Ghost Towns of the Colorado Rockies
ISBN 0-87004-342-0
6x9, 401 pages, 136 photos, map, index, $17.95

Jeep Trails to Colorado Ghost Towns
ISBN 0-87004-021-9
6x9, 245 pages, 105 photos, endsheet map, $12.95

For a free Caxton catalog write to:

CAXTON PRESS
312 Main Street
Caldwell, ID 83605-3299

or

Visit our Internet Website:

www.caxtonpress.com

Caxton Press is a division of The CAXTON PRINTERS, Ltd.